Daily as I Rise

Jerome N Terry

WESTBOW
PRESS®
A DIVISION OF THOMAS NELSON
& ZONDERVAN

WestBow Press books may be ordered through booksellers or by contacting:

WestBow Press
A Division of Thomas Nelson & Zondervan
1663 Liberty Drive
Bloomington, IN 47403
www.westbowpress.com
1 (866) 928-1240

ISBN: 978-1-9736-3012-8 (sc)
ISBN: 978-1-9736-3013-5 (hc)
ISBN: 978-1-9736-3011-1 (e)

Library of Congress Control Number: 2018906582

Print information available on the last page.

WestBow Press rev. date: 6/22/2018

This work is dedicated to:
My wife Dora
My children Tanya, Toosdi and Tamyra
My grandchildren: Damon, Breann, Darius
Roy, JaRai, Lyria and Amyah
My Great Grandchildren: Carter, Mason and Emery

I am Blessed by the best his name is Jesus
Christ and he has enough for you too!

Foreword

He replied, "Blessed rather are those who hear the
word of God and obey it." Luke 11:28

I was flattered when asked to write the Foreword for this devotional
book. I have been blessed in receiving devotions from this author for
many years. I know the author better than most and can call him
by many names, friend, prayer partner, confidant, Christian, Pastor.
However, with much pride, I choose to call him brother today. Not only
because, he is my biological brother but because he is also my brother
in Christ. His writings and teaching is God-Inspired. Before the
beginning of time God knew Lula and Noyd Terry would be married
and their first born would become an ordained Pastor, write a book
and their third born would have the honor of writing the foreword.

As siblings throughout our lives we have disagreed, agreed, and shared
a lot of good times, hard times, ups and downs. In everything and
through everything we never stopped loving, caring and encouraging
each other. That's why I am able to say I am proud of my brother. Proud
that he put to pen what The Holy Spirit placed in his heart, proud of
the fact he loves the LORD; proud that we share the desire to speak,
teach, and write God's Word. Lastly, proud of the fact this book is an
excellent way to commune with God through these devotions. People
get ready to be blessed by a life-changing Word; to see the scriptures
revealed to you in clarity and truth, Devine revelation, and increased
knowledge of the fullness of Christ.

Jerome's loving Sister,
Pamela Terry Bornes

Daily as I Rise

(Psalm 63:1KJV) O God, thou art my God; early will I seek thee: my soul thirsteth for thee, my flesh longeth for thee in a dry and thirsty land, where no water is.

Each day as I rise to a new day given me by the Lord God Almighty, my first thoughts are of him. As my eyes open to behold the new day my first offering to him is a praise of thanksgiving for allowing me another opportunity to carry on in the work he has called me to do. As the word of God illustrates to us the work of God is to believe in the one whom he sent, Jesus the Christ (**John 6:29**). These devotions and prayers may be used as a guide for your daily worship and prayed for yourself individually or you may use them for those around you. Use them as a guide to ignite praise in your daily life as you seek God early each morning.

Day 1

No one can come to me unless the Father who sent me draws him, and I will raise him up at the last day. John 6:44 (NIV)

No person can come into the presence of Jesus under his own volition. This is an act of God coming into the heart of a person and directing them to place their faith in Christ Jesus as their Lord and savior. God is always at work accomplishing this good work in the lives of everyday people. There are those who have heard of the Lord Jesus Christ yet are not drawn to him because the work which God the father himself must complete in that person has not yet taken place.

Prayer: Father God in Heaven through you I have come to know Jesus as the Lord of my life. Thank you for the redemption which comes through him which will one day deliver me into his presence in eternal glory. Father in Jesus' name I pray this. Amen

Day 2

And this is my prayer: that your love may abound
more and more in knowledge and depth of insight.
(Philippians1:9 NIV)

God has given us a world which has many good things associated with
it. There is the Sun of the day light hours and the stars and Moon of
the night. God created this earth for his creation and mankind to live
on and enjoy. The depressing things of this world did not come from
God but through mankind's misuse of what God created. Everything
God has created is good.

Prayer: Holy Lord my Father God, give me the spiritual insight to see
the glorious goodness you have given to us in this world. Help me focus
on the positive and help me invoke change regarding the negative. Give
my heart praise for you and the majesty you intended for this life we
live. Through Christ Jesus the giver of life I pray this. Amen

Day 3

For if you forgive others their trespasses, your heavenly
Father will also forgive you. (Matthew 6:14 NRSV)

Perhaps one of the most difficult things for the human heart to
accomplish is to forgive. When we perceive hurt from another person
many times we languish in that pain and it then become difficult to
offer forgiveness to the person who harmed us. We can forgive if we
turn our hearts over to God and the power of his grace.

Prayer: Heavenly Father God, as we proceed into this new day of our
lives help us to forget the hurts of yesterday and offer forgiveness to
those who have wounded us. Give us the spirit of reconciliation as we
seek forgiveness for those acts where we caused hurt. In Jesus' name
I pray this. Amen

Day 4

For this cause we also, since the day we heard it, do not cease to pray for you, and to desire that ye might be filled with the knowledge of his will in all wisdom and spiritual understanding. (Colossians 1:9 KJV)

God has instilled in each individual person at birth the ability to understand the difference between what is right and what is wrong. We each come into this life with a clean slate and then upon that slate life begins to etch its axiom's which are brought to us by means of those whose paths cross ours in this world. Many of the things we learn in life about living are the interpretation of other individuals who believe them to be true. Truth is found only in the knowledge and wisdom which comes from the Triune God above.

Prayer: Father God in Heaven, we ask for spiritual discernment of the truths of your word. As your Word reveals to us your thoughts for mankind, enable us to follow joyfully and confidently the path which is laid out before us. Through Christ Jesus who followed the path to the cross we ask this. Amen

Day 5

I can do all things through Christ who strengthens me. (Philippians 4:13 NKJV)

We like to think that we have the ability and potency to accomplish all that we choose to do under our own strength, but the truth is that all power comes from our Lord. Our bodies are but a fragile vessel which begins the process of deterioration from the day we are born. When we submit to the Lord Jesus Christ we then experience his power flowing through us to accomplish what we in our impotence have not the capacity to accomplish.

Prayer: Comforting Savior Christ Jesus strengthen your people in all things. Only through you can we accomplish anything we attempt. We thank you. In your name we pray. Amen

Day 6

Hear my cry, O God, listen to my prayer (Psalm 61:1 NIV)

If we do not have the love of God in our hearts, we find our hearts empty. It is so very easy in this world in which we live to allow the dialogue of the ungodly to displace the word of God if that word is not firmly rooted into the very fabric of our existence. Calling continually the Lord in prayer helps us to remain rooted.

Prayer: Merciful Father God in Heaven, hear my cry as I come to you bringing my empty heart begging you to fill it with your love. Help me gracious God to be what you want me to be. Fill me with your Holy Spirit to give me direction as I seek to live in the light of your word. Through Christ Jesus I pray. Amen

Day 7

How many are my iniquities and my sins? Make me know my transgression and my sin. (Job 13:23 NJKV)

Mankind tends to cast a blind eye on its sinful activities. In fact, we sin so frequently we now view those sins as minor indiscretions for which we are not held accountable. We no longer view a rude word as sin. We no longer view a wandering eye as sin. We covet and view it as ambition. Only as we view our activities under the light of God's word can we see sin for what it truly is, sin.

Prayer: Merciful Father God in Heaven, forgive my many sins. Cleanse me of my iniquity. Enable me to bear my cross in faithful adherence to discipleship. Help me to follow Christ Jesus through whom I pray. Amen

Day 8

This is the day that the Lord has made; let us rejoice
and be glad in it. (Psalm 118:24 NIV)

Each day as we arise anew we see that God has given us another
opportunity on this earth to again accomplish his purpose in our life
and the lives of those with whom we come in contact. Each new day is
God given and precious. Ask God's guidance as you move through the
day. Use it wisely and squander it not.

Prayer: Almighty Father God, today I move into something I have
never seen before, a new day. Take my hand precious Lord and guide
me where you want me to go. Speak to my heart and give me comfort
as I walk the un-traveled path of life. Through Christ Jesus I pray this.
Amen

Day 9

And Jesus went on with his disciples to the villages of
Caesarea Philippi. And on the way he asked his disciples,
"Who do people say that I am?" (Mark 8:27 ESV)

Knowledge is power. You have heard this phrase before. True knowledge
is first given from God above. That knowledge manifests itself in the
knowledge that there is one greater than yourself through whom you
were created. The world and the fullness there of was created through
Jesus the Son of God who is God in human flesh.

Prayer: Almighty Father God, give to all the knowledge given to the
apostle Peter when asked by Christ "who do men say that I am"? Give
all peoples to know that he is the Christ, the son of the living God who
came that all men could be saved. Your word Father says that you wish
that none be lost. Through Christ Jesus I pray. Amen

Day 10

If I must boast, I will boast of the things that show my weakness. (2 Corinthians 11:30 (NIV)

God our Father is ever present to keep and protect us. We are like the weak little lambs that easily fall prey to the ravenous wolves of this world. But our Good Shepherd watches over us and he never sleeps or slumbers. We in and of ourselves are weak our strength is found in him. He says to us in our weakness do not worry "I am the Good Shepherd" who lays down his life for his sheep".

Prayer: Heavenly Father God, there is so much evil in this world. Protect me in my weakness. Be ever near me Lord as I go through this life. Keep me and my loved ones safe from all hurt, harm and danger. Lord God Heavenly Father, rebuke and detain the adversary and all his followers in all their efforts against your people. Through Christ Jesus I have the victory and through him I pray. Amen

Day 11

Draw near to God, and he will draw near to you. Cleanse your hands, you sinners, and purify your hearts, you double-minded. (James 4:8 NKJV)

God desires to be close to you. God pursues you constantly to be in your presence. God wants to be a part of your daily life. He seeks an invitation from you. For him to reside in your inner parts the body is to be kept clean of impurity. Our thoughts, words and deeds are what we must monitor. For us this is impossible but with the help of our Lord we can clean up our act to present our bodies as a temple worthy of God's presence.

Prayer: Gracious and Eternal Lord God, the creator of heaven and earth, please let each day bring me closer to you. Live within me and do your holy work. Let me not be proud and selfish. Always help me to keep the focus on you. Through Christ Jesus I pray. Amen

Day 12

Remember for my good, O my God, all that I have done
for this people. (Nehemiah 5:19 NRSV)

We are God's creation who cohabitate with billions of other human beings on this planet earth. Because of the goodness of God found in the love shown us through Christ Jesus we should want to aid and assist one another to show God our appreciation for the love, grace and mercy shown us. Let us take note of how we interact with one another. This is God's will for us. We should want to help and not harm, raise up and not put down.

Prayer: O God our Heavenly Father, remember us and help us to continue to do good for one another while we are here on this earth. Let us help and not harm, but to lift and not put down. Help us to give all that is good to one another. In the name of Jesus, we ask this. Amen

Day 13

For we know him who said, "Vengeance is mine; I will
repay." And again, "The Lord will judge his people."
(Hebrews 10:30 NIV)

"I am going to get you for this". How many times has this thought, or these words passed through your mind and mouth? We do not feel like a man or a woman if we do not set the record straight by getting even for an infraction committed by another human being. When we succumb to revenge we try to take the place of God who is judge over all the earth. Vengeance is the Lord's. He alone has the right to judge and invoke punishment on his creation. There is nothing more dreadful than the punishment inflicted by God on the heads of sinners.

Prayer: Through your Spirit, Father God of Heaven, please empower me to be patient for you to right injustices committed against me. Please help me to be more concerned about the salvation of those who may have wronged me than I am about getting even. Please give me more of a heart like your Son, Jesus, in whose name I pray. Amen

Day 14

As each has received a gift, use it to serve one another, as
good stewards of God's varied grace. (1 Peter 4:10 ESV)

God in his graciousness has gifted everyone with either single or multiple gifts to be used in the service of kingdom building. With the diversity of gifting when we come together as the body of Christ, we then pool these talents to strive towards a mutual goal. God has given each person an identifiable gift. For some it is writing, math, electronics, mechanical aptitudes, drawing, singing, preaching, teaching, sweeping, horticulture, cleaning, arts and crafts and there is a myriad of other gifts which come from the Lord. His greatest gift to us is the gift of life. The life we have we can share with people in this world to warm their hearts with love and affection.

Prayer: Heavenly Father God, all that we own comes from you. You have given the gift of life, the possession of goods, the comfort of love. certain talents and the security of the cross. Help us to be good stewards of all you have given us. Give us a spirit of sharing that we may also share all you have given with others. In Jesus' name I pray this. Amen

Day 15

A generous man will prosper; he who refreshes others
will himself be refreshed. (Proverbs 11:25 NIV)

Many people have resources enough to provide for themselves and their families existence. Although we often have barely enough it is still enough to share with those who have nothing. We all have something we can share with others in need. If we had a family of four and each had a cup of soup and there was a person who came to your door who had no soup, if each person shares a little from their cup then all five could have soup. No matter how meager our circumstance there is enough to help someone else who has nothing. When you do this, God who sees your generous heart will prosper you with more resources.

Prayer: Gracious God our Father, giver of all good things. Bless us that we may be a blessing to others. Help us to pour out from within ourselves the grace, love, and caring you have bestowed upon us, into the lives of all whom we meet in life. Father let Christ's light and love radiate through our being and cast light and warmth into this dim, cold world. In Jesus' name we pray. Amen

Day 16

> It is because of him that you are in Christ Jesus, who has become for us wisdom from God--that is, our righteousness, holiness and redemption.
> (1 Corinthians 1:30 NIV)

Through the Lord God almighty we have been brought to our Lord Jesus Christ the savior of mankind. God had given us opportunity to be in concord with Christ. God the Father has given us the opportunity to have a relationship with Christ. In having this interaction with our Lord and savior Jesus Christ we have relationship with the God of creation, for it was Christ Jesus who created all that is, was and is ever to be. Our Lord and our God in his divinity meets us in our humanity so that we may join him one day in eternity.

Prayer: Lord God, the Great IAM who is our Creator and Father, all honor and glory, belongs to you and to our Lord and Savior Jesus Christ and to the Holy Ghost. We approach you in the name of Jesus through whom you have given us life. Holy Father we thank you for the wisdom which we have through Christ. We thank you for the sanctification which Christ Jesus brought. And we praise you for the redemption found in Christ Jesus in whom we place our faith. Thank you, we pray in Jesus' Holy and precious name. Amen

Day 17

³⁵ Who shall separate us from the love of Christ? Shall trouble or hardship or persecution or famine or nakedness or danger or sword? ³⁶ As it is written: "For your sake we face death all day long; we are considered as sheep to be slaughtered." ³⁷ No, in all these things we are more than conquerors through him who loved us. (Romans 8:35-37 NIV)

There is nothing in all of creation which can separate us from the love of our God. The trials and troubles of this life serve to bring us closer to the one who can comfort us in times of trouble. It is pain, suffering, agony and grief which lead us to embrace the Lord. It is danger, torment, and stress which embolden us to call on the name that is above every name, Jesus. Our Lord Jesus has gone through the heavens and yet lived among us on the earth, so he understands the troubles of this life. Our comfort is found in him.

Prayer: Lord God almighty and Everlasting Father. You are forever faithful in that no matter the situation you are there during the event, ever remaining close to your people. Thank you, O faithful Father God that you allow nothing on this earth, in the heavens, or anything under the earth to separate us from the love you have for us. In Jesus' name we pray. Amen

Day 18

Come to me, all who labor and are heavy laden, and I will give you rest. (Matthew 11:28 ESV)

In our daily lives we labor under the heavy burden of sin. This sin causes us to struggle against it, to find peace for our troubled souls. We cannot relieve ourselves of the burden under our own power. Because of the very nature of Jesus, he invites us to come to him. It is for this very reason he came into the earth to offer to his people rest from the burden of sin's hefty weight. All the people of this world are heavy laden with sin. There is no distinction in the seriousness of one's sin; it is not measured. Sin is sin and causes a burden upon the soul of mankind. This is a gracious invitation to the weary masses that inhabit this planet. The Savior offers us peace for the sin sick soul.

Prayer: Omnipotent God our Heavenly Father, you reign supreme over the universe, yet you are mindful of us your hand made people. Despite our vast numbers as inhabitants on this earth you come to each of us individually and you know even the very hairs of our heads. What an awesome God you are. Thank you for the rest we have from our labor which is found in Jesus Christ our Savior. In Jesus' name we pray. Amen

Day 19

> For the word of God is quick, and powerful, and sharper than any two-edged sword, piercing even to the dividing asunder of soul and spirit, and of the joints and marrow, and is a discerner of the thoughts and intents of the heart. (Hebrews 4:12 KJV)

The incarnate WORD, our Lord Jesus revealed God's written word as truth. God's written word which was divinely inspired to be written by men who God created gives us a gauge by which we can determine whether we are going to be living according to God's divine purpose for his people. The word of God gives life, yet it also exterminates. It was at the word of God that the earth and all that is on, in and above it was created. It was at the word of God that the Israelites fell in the desert after being delivered from Egypt. The words of God lay bare the thoughts and intentions of the heart of his people. The Word of God leads his people who believe in the Incarnate Word down the path to salvation.

Prayer: Father God in Heaven, your word has been prepared for us your people as a guide to living in harmony with one another and with you, while we are here on this sphere called earth. Father we live in a place and time where we can take the instruction of your word and allow it to carve away the decay which the world has grafted onto our persons. Father your quick and powerful word guides us in discerning where our hearts are leading us. Help us to absorb your word so that the intents of our hearts may be found favorable by you for the sake of our Lord and savior Jesus Christ. In Jesus' name we ask this. Amen.

Day 20

> And it shall come to pass that everyone who calls on the name of the Lord shall be saved. For in Mount Zion and in Jerusalem there shall be those who escape, as the Lord has said, and among the survivors shall be those whom the Lord calls. (Joel 2:32 ESV)

There is a name upon which we may call; a name that has and will throughout eternity be the name of him who saves his people. Calling on the name of the Lord presumes knowledge of him who is, who was and who is to come. You only call on the person you know. We never call on a stranger unless you find yourself in a dismal situation where you see no way out. When you call on the Lord you then express that you have faith that he can accomplish for you what you need done. In calling on the Lord you indicate your submission to him which reflects your dependence on him for relief from your situation.

Prayer: Father God as we experience the trials and tribulations of life we thank you that you have offered us the opportunity to call on your name. Holy and Gracious Father God our IAM. Thank you for saving our physical bodies in times of danger and our souls from being lost in eternity. Thank you through our Lord Jesus for the future which awaits us in the place prepared by Christ Jesus for eternity. Father we praise you in your fullness. This we pray in the name of the Father, Son and Holy Spirit. Amen

Day 21

fear not, for I am with you; be not dismayed, for I
am your God; I will strengthen you, I will help you,
I will uphold you with my righteous right hand.
(Isaiah 41:10 ESV)

How very often we feel as if we have been ridden all day long by our adversary the Devil? When Satan comes in like a rushing flood it is difficult to make a stand in your individual might against the onrush of his attack. We can in times like those look up to get hooked up to the source of strength which revitalizes our weakened condition. Our God speaks to us the words "fear not, for I am with you". When we have God in our presence we are protected by the one who loves us with a love which causes him to offer his very own life for us. Knowing the Lord God is ever present offers strength in difficult time.

Prayer: Strengthen me, O God that I may stand against Satan my foe and triumph by the power of your Spirit. Strengthen me so that I may bring honor and glory to my conquering Savior Jesus who will return one day and take me home in victory. In the name of the victorious Rider on the White Horse Jesus Christ I pray. Amen.

Day 22

Then the channels of the sea were seen, and the
foundations of the world were laid bare at your rebuke,
O Lord, at the blast of the breath of your nostrils.
(Psalm 18:15 ESV)

The God we serve is the same God who with a blast of his nostrils caused the sea to part and the Hebrews children were able to cross on dry land. This is the God who knew you while you were yet in your mother's womb. There is nothing we can hide from God he is omniscient. This is the same God who opened the womb of the earth and brought forth the flood waters in ancient time when Noah and his family were the only survivors on the ark. This is also the same God who wishes you to lay bare your soul as you come with a repentant heart earnestly seeking his forgiveness which is found in Christ Jesus. He is awesome and yet loving. He is God. As the sea bed was laid bare before him lay bare your shortcomings.

Prayer: Father God, help to lay bare my life before you. I know you know everything about me, yet I ask that I have the willingness to impart my deepest and darkest secrets. Help me to live in the purifying light of truth that is of you. Through Jesus the truth and the life I pray this. Amen

Day 23

God is spirit, and those who worship him must worship
in spirit and truth. (John 4:24 NKJV)

The God we serve is beyond the temporal inclinations of mankind. We serve an incomprehensible God. God is far beyond that of human comprehension. God is spirit, man is flesh and blood. God is eternal, man is temporal. Because God is Spirit we do not have to come into a certain place or mindset. Our God's very nature is omnipresent therefore he is in all places, always. We Must worship in spirit and truth. We must revere our eternal all powerful, loving and merciful God. He is the God of reality, fidelity, concord and love. How can we not worship him?

Prayer: Come Holy Spirit of God the creator. Help the Father's creation to worship him in spirit and truth. Help the people learn and grow. Thank you for the men and women of God who are directing God's precious people to place him first in worship and in all things. Help us all to follow you faithfully as we move closer to eternity. Through Jesus Christ we pray. Amen

Day 24

And Jesus answered and said to him, "Get behind Me, Satan! For it is written, 'You shall worship the LORD your God, and Him only you shall serve.' (Luke 4:8 NKJV)

Our works are contaminated with the impurity of pride. Regardless of what we attempt to accomplish in the name of what is right, true and good, we diminish it by a lack of complete humility in our hearts. In knowing this we see Christ Jesus at work in our lives just as he was at work over two thousand years ago. While we were still sinners he died for us. He died to redeem us from the deficiency of the flesh which cannot under its own power accomplish anything which is good. Our Spirit directed living is our attempt to offer worship to our Lord and our God.

Prayer: Father God, there are times when we go in the wrong direction even in attempting to serve you. Thank you for saving us despite ourselves. Thank you for your grace and mercy. Thank you for the loving care you give through the Holy Spirit. Give us wisdom to faithfully follow you in all things. Through Christ Jesus we pray. Amen

Day 25

I have sent him to you for this very purpose, that you may know how we are, and that he may encourage your hearts. (Ephesians 6:22 ESV)

Our Father God will often use the hands of other people to fulfill his purpose in our lives. There will be times when other people will damage you and break your hearts, but Our god has another person waiting to be the hands of Christ which come to soothe and comfort the broken hearted. The same hands which were nailed to the cross of Calvary are the hands of the Father, mother, sister or brother whose gentle touch gives us that much needed comfort in times of trouble.

Prayer: Holy Father, comfort us when our fragile hearts are broken by the acts of fellow human beings. O God give us the comfort found that Christ Jesus won for us on the cross of Calvary. Through Jesus we ask this. Amen

Day 26

Wash me thoroughly from my iniquity, and cleanse me from my sin! (Psalm 51:2 KJV)

Sin is ever before us; we wallow in it from the womb to the tomb. We are encumbered with an inherent condition from which we cannot escape. We act out involuntarily as we manifest our inherited nature in thought, word and deed. We cannot help ourselves. But when the time was right Christ Jesus came to save us from sin's condemnation. It is the blood of Christ Jesus which cleanses us from sin.

Prayer: Holy Father, in the name of Jesus, cleanse us of all our sin. Wash our sin sick souls and remove the darkness found in them. Heavenly Father give us clean hearts to be used in your service. Through Jesus our redeemer we ask this. Amen

Day 27

Help us, O God of our salvation, For the glory of Your name; And deliver us, and provide atonement for our sins, For Your name's sake! (Psalm 79:9 NKJV)

We pray to the Lord our God in the name of Jesus to help us in times of need. It is very interesting that this is the time when many who do not regularly pray bow their heads and ask God through Christ to intervene in the situations they find themselves in. This indicates that deep down in the soul of mankind there is a groping for a power beyond themselves which they know can be tapped into. The sadness is that it takes trouble to bring people to this point of realization.

Prayer: Holy Lord God, help us children of men to keep our focus on Jesus. Give us the patience of faith as we await his return. Enable us to spread the good news to all who would receive it, that your word may be proclaimed throughout the land. In Jesus' precious name we pray this. Amen

Day 28

> But now in Christ Jesus you who once were far off have been brought near by the blood of Christ. (Ephesians 2:13 NIV)

Sin is always waiting at the door of our hearts to enter and carry us along with it towards its pursuits. We must be ever mindful of how we interact with this world. All around us are the trappings of sin; we often become immersed in sin's mire before we even realize it. Our media, music and literature carry us down the paths of sin. We must guard ourselves through prayer and be watchful.

Prayer: Almighty Loving Father God, I give you thanks for the cleansing blood of Jesus which was poured out at Calvary for the forgiveness of my sin and the sins of all. Thank you that no other sacrifice is necessary. Through Christ Jesus the Lamb who was slain we pray. Amen

Day 29

> Come to me, all who labor and are heavy laden, and I will give you rest. (Matthew 11:28 ESV)

We carry on our shoulders great burdens. We have the responsibility of providing for our families and loved ones. We have the responsibility of loyalty to our country and employer. We have the responsibility of being true to one's self. People, places and things lay such great demands on us we cannot accomplish them all. We try until we are worn down, then we come to the realization that we are only human and as a human being we have limitations. We can only then seek rest from our labor in the embrace of our Lord.

Prayer: Almighty and Everlasting Father God, there are times in this life when we find ourselves in situations that are beyond our control. It is times like those that we ask that your Holy Spirit encourage us to cast our cares on you. You say come to you those who are burdened, and you will give them rest. Father take our cares and woes and give us peace as only you can give peace. Through Christ Jesus who brought us peace with you we ask this. Amen

Day 30

but no human being can tame the tongue. It is a restless evil, full of deadly poison. (James 3:8 ESV)

How many times have you thought to yourself "I wish I had not said that"? Our tongues can be venomous as we speak to other human beings. Even the people we love often fall victim to our tongue. What is stored up in the hearts finds its way to the mouth and the words are then formed by the tongue which spews them out in a torrent of insults, curses and ill will. We must persistently seek to manage our tongue.

Prayer: God of grace, forgive us for our mismanaged tongue which speaks hurtful words into the lives of those around us. Please, Father God heal those wounds which have been inflicted. Give us a voice of healing not of harm. Through Christ Jesus we pray this. Amen

Day 31

By the sweat of your face you shall eat bread, till you return to the ground, for out of it you were taken; for you are dust, and to dust you shall return. (Genesis 3:19 NKJV)

In this life we must work long and hard. Typically, we work at a job for thirty or forty years as we move towards retirement. You work day after day to provide the necessities of life. We toil for food, shelter and clothing until one day we end our existence on this earth by keeping the appointment all mankind must keep which is death. We will one day be changed back to the dust from which mankind originated. However, while living we engage in activities which sustain life, corrupt life and finally end life.

Prayer: Holy God, Gracious Lord God Father Almighty, Everlasting Eternal God, God of Mercy forgive me for my sins of commission and for my sins of omission. I am but dust from the earth and to that dust I shall return. Cleanse me loving God of that which defiles me. In Jesus' name I pray. Amen

Day 32

> but if you do not forgive others their trespasses, neither will your Father forgive your trespasses. (Matthew 6:15 ESV)

To include anger, indignation and hurt, is one of the most difficult accomplishments of the human consciousness where forgiveness is the order of the day. We want our pound of flesh for perceived infractions against our property, loved ones and person. Upon close examination as we hold onto our resentments we find that the only person suffering is the person who cannot forgive. Usually the other person has moved on in life, yet we become so consumed with condemnation that we find ourselves poisoned by it. God through Christ Jesus forgives over and over, sometimes for the same offense. We should examine our actions and emulate God in the act of forgiveness.

Prayer: Forgiving Father God, help me to be mindful of the patience and forgiveness you give towards me repeatedly. Lead me to be patient with those whom I interact with as I work towards forgiveness in my heart towards my perceived hurt. In Jesus' name I pray. Amen

Day 33

> You shall remember the Lord your God, for it is he who
> gives you power to get wealth, that he may confirm his
> covenant that he swore to your fathers, as it is this day.
> (Deuteronomy 8:18 ESV)

As we walk through life we seek after the toys this world has to offer. Our society seems to dictate that he who finishes with the most toys is that one who has succeeded in life. We strive after cars, clothes, houses, jewels and money. After all the worldly striving we find that the promise of fulfillment is still not satisfied. But if we use those earthly possessions for the benefit of God's people then we find satisfaction in them.

Prayer: Heavenly Father God, all that we own come from you. You have given the gift of life, the possession of goods, the comfort of love and the security of the cross. Help us to be good stewards of all you have given us. Give us a spirit of sharing that we may also share all you have given with others. In Jesus' name we pray. Amen

Day 34

> But we see Jesus, who was made a little lower than the
> angels, now crowned with glory and honor because he
> suffered death, so that by the grace of God he might
> taste death for everyone. (Hebrews 2:9 NIV)

God had placed everything in the care of mankind, the birds of the air, the beasts of the fields and the fish of the sea. Man lost that position through disobedience. Mankind is restored through Christ Jesus to the position that God intended as he created man to have dominion over his creation earth. Jesus is the only man who could accomplish this. It is through Jesus' obedience to living a perfect life; dying an ignominious death not for his sins but for ours. He took our sins upon himself; although innocent he suffered that we can receive redemption as he carried our iniquities to the cross of Calvary. Through this selfless act one future day we will reign in sovereignty over creation again.

Prayer: Heavenly Father, we are guilty of defiling your gifts of grace, mercy, love and life. Help us to remember the bitter suffering of Jesus and confess individually and corporately our sin. Hear our confession and see in us only, your son who bore our burdens to Calvary. In Jesus' name I pray. Amen

Day 35

> But You, O GOD the Lord, Deal with me for Your name's sake; Because Your mercy is good, deliver me. (Psalm 109:21 NKJV)

As a young child seeks the nearness of its parents we too want the nearness of our Father God. As a child you can remember being held by your parents with the security this offered you. While we walk the path of life we do not always feel we are in the presence of our Father God. It is at those lonely times that the weight of the worlds seems to come crashing down upon our shoulders. We seek the peace of God which surpasses all understanding for our tranquility.

Prayer: Holy and Almighty God, I come to you in my pitiful state seeking your embrace. As your child, I seek your nearness. I seek the security of your love. I wish to hear you speak to me through your word, which gives me tranquility as I know you are near. I seek the cross which gives me eternity in your presence. I thank you Father that you allow me to seek you and find you through Jesus my Lord and savior who died to bring me into right relationship with you. In Jesus' name I pray this. Amen

Day 36

> We were buried therefore with him by baptism into death, in order that, just as Christ was raised from the

dead by the glory of the Father, we too might walk in
newness of life. (Romans 6:4 ESV)

Our old Adam or our sinful man is buried with baptism and the new man spiritually born into the body of Christ Jesus appears renewed into the world. Through this act of faith, we then are made privileged to God's amazing grace as we are joined with Christ. Through this newness of life, we must seek to cast off sin, rejecting those things which cause discord in the body of Christ and had once alienated us from fellowship with God our Father.

Prayer: Heavenly Father God, we praise our Lord Jesus Christ for the cleansing water of Baptism which for Christians allows them to die to sin. Thank you for the empty tomb of Christ Jesus which demonstrates that as he was raised from death so shall we be raised when he returns to carry us to that prepared place he has for his prepared people. Knowing what lies ahead for us merciful Father, help us to walk in the newness of life which Christ Jesus brings. In Jesus' name we pray. Amen

Day 37

Do you not know that if you present yourselves to
anyone as obedient slaves, you are slaves of the one
whom you obey, either of sin, which leads to death,
or of obedience, which leads to righteousness?
(Romans 6:16 ESV)

If you obey the directives of the sinful nature, then you have sold yourselves to sin and then you become its slave carrying out its instructions without recourse. Life gives us choices as does our God who will under no circumstance impose his will on you. Therefore, you have a decision to make "This day, whom shall you serve"?

Prayer: Our Father in Heaven, we present ourselves to you in total obedience. Help us to feel compelled in our Spirits to continue performing that work which Christ began in his ministry before his ascension. Help us to share your love with one another as a sign that we are held by you and serve you as obedient servants. Help us to obey your will which leads to righteousness and reject sin which leads to the second death. In Jesus' name we pray this. Amen

Day 38

and I will be a father to you, and you shall be sons
and daughters to me, says the Lord Almighty.
(2 Corinthians 6:18 ESV)

Without the benefit of the seed of an earthly father not one of us would exist on earth. Yet our earthly fathers can in some cases not be the biological father of our birth. A father is the provider for his children and this provision extends from physical to spiritual. God our creator Father speaks to us saying he is our Father in Heaven. We out of gratitude and reverence must never degrade this relationship. Through God our Father we receive felicity, provision, hope and salvation. Our Father which is in Heaven we are grateful for your love.

Prayer: O God thank you for the relationship you have given us as sons and daughters through our Lord and Savior Jesus Christ. Through him we will be received when we come into your house. And through him in your house you have a place prepared for us. Thank you for caring for us despite our rebellious nature. Through Christ Jesus we pray. Amen

Day 39

If I give all I possess to the poor and surrender my
body to the flames, but have not love, I gain nothing.
(1 Corinthians 13:3 NIV)

As the Lord God Almighty offers to each of us individually and collectively love, despite our continued rejection of him as we sin in thought, word and deed. Let us take up the mantle of mutual care for each other out of the manifestation of the love given us. We can choose to walk in darkness or we can move into the glorious light of God's love which we can share with this world.

Prayer: Almighty and Everlasting Father God remove our prideful character and enable us to surrender to your loving care. Thank you for forgiving us as we reject the care you continually offer us while we still exist on this sphere called earth. Deliver us from the power of darkness into the marvelous light of life which comes through Christ our Savior. Through Jesus I ask this. Amen

Day 40

> By this we know love, that he laid down his life for us,
> and we ought to lay down our lives for the brothers.
> (1 John 3:16 ESV)

Our great God has given his very human life for our redemption that we, through his death may be reconciled back to him as those who are his are now saved from condemnation through his sacrificial act. The question today is who would you be willing to lay down your life for?

Prayer: God of Love, help us to display love to one another. You showed your love for us through Christ at Calvary. Enable us to show our love for you by loving one another. Help us to love especially the unlovable, for what does it benefit us to love those who love us. Help us father God. In Jesus' name I pray. Amen

Day 41

> But you are a chosen generation, a royal priesthood,
> a holy nation, His own special people, that you may
> proclaim the praises of Him who called you out of
> darkness into His marvelous light. (1 Peter 2:9 NKJV)

Our God who created the Heavens and the Earth has chosen you as his people. He knew you before you were ever conceived in your mother's womb. He desires that you believe in him through Christ Jesus God incarnate. Reject impure thought, immoral activity and unclean speech. Move out of a life in the shadows into a life illuminated with the radiance of a life filled with Christ Jesus our God.

Prayer: Heavenly Father, you have called us out of the darkness of sin into the marvelous light of life by your word and through Christ. Help us not return to the sinful lifestyles which call to our carnal nature. Help us to resist the temptation of sin. In Jesus' name we ask this. Amen

Day 42

Because he holds fast to me in love, I will deliver him; I will protect him, because he knows my name. (Psalm 91:14 ESV)

To those who truly love and trust God, his never ceasing protection is there accompanying you throughout each day. God's love for us extends beyond the norm of human understanding. God's love watches over us in our waking hours and sleeping hours, when we are established in every circumstance. We have a God who comforts us in any and every trial and trouble no matter where we are in this world. Looking back at past times of trouble; knowing that it was only through the love of God that you made it through those situations. You can in faith again call on the name of the Lord for assured deliverance no matter how bleak the outlook.

Prayer: Almighty Father God, your love transcends geographic distances, politics, and human circumstances. Omnipresent God you know our needs perfectly and care about us where ever we may be. Send your Holy Spirit to comfort and guide us in our journey of faith, even as we traverse difficult and unfamiliar environments and surroundings. In Jesus' name we pray. Amen

Day 43

And there is salvation in no one else, for there is no
other name under heaven given among men by which
we must be saved. (Acts 4:12 ESV)

The movies are full of characters that come in the nick of time to save
people, the town, the nation or the world. When we were children and
we needed someone to come to our aid we called on big brother, sister,
mom or dad. In the earthly realm we still call on others to come to our
aid and save us from situations we find ourselves in. For every one of
us our rescue from eternal condemnation is found only in Christ Jesus
our salvation, no one else can do this. Salvation is not found in Buddha,
Mohammed, Confucius or any other human being that has lived, is
living or who will one day live.

Prayer: Almighty and Everlasting God, thank you for the salvation
we have through Jesus. Although we are unworthy of such loving
redemption you have done for us what we could not accomplish for
ourselves. Through Christ Jesus we pray. Amen

Day 44

Jesus said to him, I am the way, and the truth, and the life. No one
comes to the Father except through me. (John 14:6 NKJV)

Unlike a computer that is password protected there is no backdoor
into heaven. For us to receive the kingdom as our eternal home
we must first place out faith in the redemption of Christ Jesus and
his sacrificial act on the cross of Calvary. God our heavenly father
sent his son Jesus Christ to die that we through his death would be
cleansed of our sins. Through his resurrection we too will one day
be raised to life and live with him forever in that prepared place he
has built for us.

Prayer: Dear giving and loving Father God, thank you for freeing us from the burden of sin's penalty. Because of Christ we can face a certain future looking forward to spending eternity with him in paradise.

Day 45

So, teach us to number our days, that we may gain a heart of wisdom. (Psalm 90:12 NKJV)

Mankind is given a determined number of days to live on this planet earth. The goal of all should be to gain wisdom as we progress in years so that those persons in our lives who experience the trials, temptations and even successes of life can gain insight from us as we have passed that way before. Our mortality is certain as we proceed from the womb to the tomb. Only a fool learns nothing in his trek through life. Only the arrogant does not wisely use the time God has given to develop a relationship with God through his son Jesus. Wisdom teaches us to ponder hardily on eternity and hold loosely to the temporal.

Prayer: O LORD God Almighty, please give us wisdom and courage to see your will for our life. In Jesus' name we pray. Amen

Day 46

Know therefore that the Lord your God is God; he is the faithful God, keeping his covenant of love to a thousand generations of those who love him and keep his commands. (Deuteronomy 7:9 NIV)

God is real! The God of the Bible is illustrated as the God who created all animals, plants, humans and substances. In his creating God did so in a way that he provided for the needs of his entire creation. When corruption came to the creation God then provided a means of salvation, which would occur down through the generations in the form of his coming to earth as the incarnate God. The day is coming when he will return to carry all who are his to a prepared place for his prepared people.

Prayer: Dear Loving Father God, we come to you in the name of Jesus asking that you give us the comfort that comes only from your loving care. Help us to trust that you are faithful in your promise to receive us despite all our cares and woes. Heal us where healing is needed either spiritually, physically, financially or mentally. This we ask in Jesus' name. Amen

Day 47

> For if any be a hearer of the word, and not a doer, he is like unto a man beholding his natural face in a glass. (James 1:23 KJV)

The word of God as found in his book the Bible is a blueprint for living a life which offers peace, love, compassion and harmony, in this world. Mankind does not live in harmony because each person exists on selfish rationale. This is a world of me, me, me. Society has been taught to focus on self and because of that it is every man for himself. When we allow our actions to be guided by the word of God we can live harmoniously with one another without the desire to cause harm as we focus on us, us, us. The Word of God teaches love for others and that type of love is not self-seeking.

Prayer: Loving Father God, help us each day to live out your word. By the power of your Holy Spirit empower us to be doers of your word while we are yet on this side of the cross. In Jesus' Holy and precious name, we pray. Amen

Day 48

> Therefore, confess your sins to each other and pray for each other so that you may be healed. The prayer of a righteous man is powerful and effective. (James 5:16 NIV)

We want. This is the nucleus of most prayer as we look inward ever wanting more and yet more. Our prayers often suggest our self-centered requests of a God who we want to do for us what we want done as we want it done. When we do not consider what God has given we tend to think he has withheld many blessings. But if we just take the time to look at our lives we can view how much God has given throughout the course of our lives. When we assess what he has given this should encourage us to ask blessings for others, especially that Christ comes into their lives.

Prayer: O God in Heaven, all too often our prayers are those which ask for the desires of our hearts. Teach us to pray beyond our selves for those around us. Help our prayers to be for those who have yet to know Christ and he crucified. In Jesus' Holy and precious name, we pray. Amen

Day 49

He replied, "Whether he is a sinner or not, I don't know. One thing I do know. I was blind but now I see!" (John 9:25 NIV)

In our weakness we lash out at others to qualify and support our position in life. Where we find weakness or a chink in the armor of another we take advantage of it. God is the God of all people and we all need him equally. Let us reach out with the open hand of friendship offering aid to one another. Let us refrain from offering the closed fist of conflict to bludgeon one another into submission.

Prayer: Dear LORD God Almighty, we children of men are but weak vessels which rely solely upon your favor for all our needs. Give us spiritual sight that we may view others as your children and offer to them the grace, mercy and compassion which came from you and the cross of Christ Jesus. Help us to speak as the man who was blind from birth then healed by Christ. "I was blind but now I see". In Jesus' name we pray. Amen

Day 50

God is faithful, by whom you were called into
the fellowship of his Son, Jesus Christ our Lord.
(1 Corinthians 1:9 NKJV)

Who can you trust? Can you even trust yourself in certain situations? If you have lived with yourself and know that there are times when you need someone else to keep you from acting out, then you are untrustworthy unto self. We lie, cheat and even steal from ourselves. Then we try to justify it by saying things like "The devil made me do it". If that be so, then your relationship is with the wrong celestial being. We can trust in the Lord God Almighty alone in this world. He alone cares for our every need and in doing so he watches over each one of his children. He never leaves us alone.

Prayer: Almighty and Sovereign LORD God of our fathers Abraham, Isaac, and Jacob. We praise you for your faithfulness to your promises. We thank you for your redemptive work through many generations. We deeply appreciate you sending your son Jesus our Messiah to redeem us. We praise you for inspiring the Scriptures to teach us your truth. Please know our deep gratitude for the blessing of belonging to you and knowing that we can trust our future with you. Please bless your people with an awesome sense of your abiding presence and use us to bring you glory. In Jesus' name we pray. Amen

Day 51

But the Lord said to Samuel, "Do not consider his
appearance or his height, for I have rejected him. The
Lord does not look at the things man looks at. Man
looks at the outward appearance, but the Lord looks
at the heart." (1 Samuel 16:7 NIV)

When we look at one another we view the outward and then base out perception of the person on what we see. When looking at the opposite gender that person may be aesthetically appealing. It is only after you get to know a person that you find the exterior does not resemble the interior. Beauty is fleeting and will certainly pass away, but the heart is a true barometer of an individual. Seek to know the heart of a person where true beauty resides.

Prayer: Almighty Father God, you know the darkness which resides in the hearts of men. You know those things which are of the adversary, bitterness, anger, discord, evil speaking. According to your will change us into the new creation which has the light of life. In Jesus' name we ask this. Amen

Day 52

> my lips will not speak wickedness, and my tongue will
> utter no deceit. (Job 27:4 NIV)

We are all God's precious children. We are alike in that we are all sinful and unclean. Neither of us has the right or the privilege to speak ill of another. We must guard carefully what we say about one another. Because as we raise our hand and point the finger at another we must remember that three fingers are pointing back towards us from that same hand. We all being lost must encourage each other to be better, do better and know better as we walk towards eternity.

Prayer: Dear Heavenly Father, help us to use our words carefully to help and not harm. Help us to not twist the truth which may harm others. Through Jesus the truth I ask this. Amen

Day 53

> A man who lacks judgment derides his neighbor,
> but a man of understanding holds his tongue.
> (Proverbs 11:12 NIV)

There are people who show openly their contempt for each other. This type of action does not lead to harmony in any relationship but nourished the fires of open conflict. If we but first seek God before interacting with a person we perceive as difficult then the ointment of tranquility can be applied by the Holy Spirit before coming into each other's presence. This balm will quench the fires of heated anger giving a refreshing serenity to the words interchanged.

Prayer: Lord God heavenly Father, thank you for being there in the difficult times. Thank you for curbing our tongues when we want to lash out. Thank you for your never-ending presence in our lives. Through Jesus I give thanks. Amen

Day 54

> All of us also lived among them at one time, gratifying the cravings of our sinful nature and following its desires and thoughts. Like the rest, we were by nature objects of wrath. (Ephesians 2:3 NIV)

How often does it seem that your focus is "I want what I want, and I want it now"? More often, than not would be the guess. This type of thinking has caused us some sort of problem as we march through life. If we had the opportunity to have things the way we independently wanted them, this would be a chaotic place to live. No two people think alike, and agreement is often difficult to reach. Only God has perfect will which is beneficial to everyone involved. Following his will, will never create conflict.

Prayer: Father God in Heaven, we your handmade servants often do things according to our desires. Lord God make your will recognizable to us and give us the power to carry it out. In Jesus' name I pray. Amen

Day 55

And he passed in front of Moses, proclaiming, The
LORD, the LORD, the compassionate and gracious
God, slow to anger, abounding in love and faithfulness.
(Exodus 34:6 NIV)

The Lord our God is Great and Mighty yet Compassionate and Merciful. We have a God who is strong and mighty, gracious, bountiful, long suffering and full of truth as He takes away our transgressions. The Lord is love and asks us to love each other with a pure undefiled love which demands no reciprocation. God although all powerful does not demand our love either for him or his creation. We should seek to emulate towards one another what God has demonstrated to us.

Prayer: Great and compassionate Father God, you renew your kindness towards us each day. Despite our character defects, despite our spiritual shortcomings, despite our lack of love for one another, you continue to care for us your wayward children. Send the Holy Spirit to help us live in accordance with your command to love one another as Christ loves us. In Jesus' name we ask this. Amen

Day 56

God is our refuge and strength, an ever-present help in
trouble. (Psalm 46:1 NIV)

We walk through this life full of toil and trouble. Some of the troubles are real and some are but phantoms of our mind. When the dark clouds of adversity billow in and shut out the shining sun of joy remember that God is there amidst the darkness guiding you through. God is only as far away as your calling on his Holy name.

Prayer: Ever Present Loving and Compassionate Father God, thank you for being ever present in our lives. There are times when we feel that we are walking through this life alone but remind us that you said never will I leave you, never will I forsake you. Thank you for also saying "Remember I am with you always". Help us to be sensitive to your Holy presence in our lives. In Jesus' name I pray. Amen

Day 57

> [4]And I prayed to the LORD my God, and made confession, and said, "O Lord, great and awesome God, who keeps His covenant and mercy with those who love Him, and with those who keep His commandments, [5] we have sinned and committed iniquity, we have done wickedly and rebelled, even by departing from Your precepts and Your judgments. (Daniel 9:4-5 NKJV)

Our God, the creator of all things is longsuffering and filled with compassion for his creation. The LORD God in his consideration of us gave his only son as a sacrifice to redeem us from our sin. God our Father is ever waiting for us to turn to him with repentant hearts which are filled with remorse, seeking his forgiveness for inappropriate actions in our lives. Because of Jesus we can confess, repent and receive forgiveness of sin. "What an Awesome God we serve".

Prayer: O Lord our Great and Awesome God. Father God we come to you in the name of Jesus thanking you for your faithfulness towards us. We have rebelled against your decrees, we have done evil to one another, yet your mercy endures, and you await our repentant heart to cry out to you asking forgiveness in Jesus' name. Please forgive our sin, for the sake of our Lord Jesus' suffering and death. There is none other like you merciful God. Bless us with repentant hearts so we may honor your grace, mercy and love for us. In Jesus' name we pray. Amen

Day 58

> Joshua said to the people, "You are not able to serve the LORD. He is a holy God; he is a jealous God. He will not forgive your rebellion and your sins. (Joshua 24:19 NIV)

Everywhere in life we encounter people who profess Christianity but upon closer examination we find them not walking the walk as they talk the talk. It is the choice of every individual whom it is they will serve. You must have your actions align with the legitimacy of God's word which gives direction for correct living. As God's people we should seek to produce internal holiness and Christ likeness in all we say, think and do. We cannot serve both God and the world. God is a jealous God so when we commit to God we must do so entirely rejecting the world.

Prayer: Holy God creator of Heaven and earth, your people are often deceived by empty words and actions of false Christians. Let the light of your truth shine its brightness on the darkness of their deception. Help your people O God to have no fellowship with the unfruitful works of darkness. Awaken them as the light of Christ illuminates their lives and awakens them from the dead and sinful activities this world offers. Through Jesus we pray this. Amen

Day 59

But in your great mercy you did not put an end to them or abandon them, for you are a gracious and merciful God. (Nehemiah 9:31 NIV)

In God's great mercy we his handmade servants who sin by what we do and who sin by what we do not, do are blessed. We are blessed because we do not receive the just punishment our actions deserve. We receive God's mercy as it is given through Christ Jesus the Lamb of God who takes away the sins of the world. Oh, how we should want to reject sin in all its forms because of his gracious mercy.

Prayer: Merciful Father God, thank you for the blessed assurance of eternal life which is found in Christ Jesus. As we advance through these Holy days of life, help your hand made creation to understand the price paid for our salvation. Give us the ability to reject selfish activity for the greater good associated with your kingdom, by truly loving and caring for one another. In Jesus' name we pray. Amen

Day 60

He remembered that they were but flesh, a passing
breeze that does not return. (Psalm 78:39 NIV)

Our Lord and our God restrains his anger against us as we walk in
iniquity. God does not destroy mankind as he once destroyed the
world with a great flood. God our redeemer sees Christ Jesus as we
come to him asking forgiveness of sins. only the power of the Holy
Spirit creates a penitent heart which feels God's wrath and compels
us to repent. Repentance brings about a new spirit filled life, the old
passes away and the new begins to take form and definition.

Prayer: Father God, all too often we attempt to speak the words of
Christianity, but our flesh presents worldly action. Help us Father God
of grace to operate in the spirit and not in the flesh. In Jesus' name I
pray. Amen

Day 61

Acknowledge and take to heart this day that the LORD
is God in heaven above and on the earth below. There
is no other. (Deuteronomy 4:39 NIV)

There is only one God and Father of the Cosmos. This is the God who
sits high and looks low seeing all that was, is, and ever shall be. This is
the God who never slumbers. This is the God who by the words of his
mouth spoke all things into existence. This is the God who has given us
his Word, both written and in the flesh to grow his kingdom through
discipleship. Let us join him by sharing his Word with those whom we
meet as he works in the lives of everyday people.

Prayer: Dear God in Heaven, help us to share your Holy Word to bless
others and bring growth to your kingdom. As your word goes forward
let it draw all men into a discipleship relationship with Christ our
Savior. Through Christ Jesus we pray. Amen

Day 62

So, if the Son sets you free, you will be free indeed.
(John 8:36 NIV)

We are slaves to sin! We are held securely in the grip of sin's entanglement. Often, we feel as if there is little hope of ever being able to overcome the burden we bear as we struggle daily with sin and its consequences. Our hope comes from Christ Jesus. When we come to him sincerely seeking forgiveness the chains of sin are then broken as the cross of Christ shatters them freeing us from condemnation.

Prayer: Lord Jesus, our hope comes from you alone. It is only through the loving act you committed at Calvary that has rescued us from eternal death. Thank you for bringing us into eternal life. Help us to emulate your love for us as we encounter other human beings, even those who have harmed us. We pray this in your name. Amen

Day 63

and as she stood behind him at his feet weeping, she
began to wet his feet with her tears. Then she wiped
them with her hair, kissed them and poured perfume
on them. (Luke 7:38 NIV)

If we are brutally honest with ourselves concerning sin, we are aware that we have been forgiven much. Like the woman who washes the Lord's feet with her tears we should seek to give evidence of our love for the Lord. We can demonstrate our love through offering forgiveness when someone offends us. We pray: "Forgive us as we forgive others". If God forgives us as we forgive where would we be?

Prayer: Father God in Heaven, today we remember the cross of Calvary and our Lord and Savior Jesus as he was hung up for our hang ups. Let the thought of that day change our lives. For many the common knowledge that our sins are forgiven no longer bring amazement.

Help us to feel outrage at our own sinful activities and present to you a contrite repentant and sorrowful heart. Allow our hearts to sorrow deeply as the woman who washed Jesus' feet with her tears. Father God thank you, for sending our salvation through Christ our Redeemer. In his name we pray. Amen

Day 64

> But when he asks, he must believe and not doubt, because he who doubts is like a wave of the sea, blown and tossed by the wind. (James 1:6 NIV)

God desires that we trust him in all things. People often fear to seek God's blessing because of the sinful nature of mankind. We know that no good thing should be given to us because of our inappropriate actions with one another. God through his blessed forgiveness which originates in Christ Jesus, desires that your life be abundant in spiritual, physical and relationship blessings.

Prayer: Father God you understand the doubts and fears of mankind. Thank you for allowing us to ask in the name of Jesus and receive as your word promises. We know that you will give us whatever we need and some of what we desire. Thank you for giving us what we need to bolster our faith that we might believe. Thank you for giving us some of our desires that we may know you as our provider. Through Jesus we pray. Amen

Day 65

> The fear of the LORD is pure, enduring forever. The ordinances of the LORD are sure and altogether righteous. (Psalm 19:9 NIV)

The most difficult thing in this world for us to accomplish is to manage our lives so they align with the will of God. We want to think that we are basically good people. When we place our supposed goodness next to the goodness of our God who created us we fail in the comparison. Because of that alone we should be in awe of God. Only God is good! God is merciful towards our shortcomings and it never fails. In our best effort all we can do is keep trying as we move towards eternity and the day of our Lord when Jesus comes to carry us home to be with him.

Prayer: Father God, we give you thanks for your enduring mercy which never fails. Because of our sinful nature we fall short and need your constant forgiveness. Through your Holy Spirit guide, us down the straight and narrow road which leads to life. In Jesus' name we pray. Amen

Day 66

No, in all these things we are more than conquerors through him who loved us. (Romans 8:37 NIV)

Life challenges us to live in this world yet remain apart from it. The world seeks to condemn our every action because it does not coincide with the ways of this world. Because we are different we are attacked by those whose father is the prince of this world. The people of the world encourage Christians to adopt what the world considers as acceptable. If not, the world seeks to persecute followers of Christ, even to the point of death. Never betray the call of Christ as this leads to the better of the two choices; which is eternal life. The world leads to eternal death.

Prayer: Thank you most gracious Father God for making us more than conquerors through Christ Jesus. As we walk towards eternity show us how to conquer our flesh; bringing it into submission to your will. In Jesus' name we pray. Amen

Day 67

This is what God the LORD says, he who created the heavens and stretched them out, who spread

out the earth and all that comes out of it, who gives
breath to its people, and life to those who walk on it.
(Isaiah 42:5 NIV)

God created this earth as a habitation for his created people. In the beginning all was in harmony and there was no discord among his creation. Satan introduced sin into the world through deception. This broke fellowship with creation and God. To restore a hint of fellowship on this earth we need to exhibit love to one another. Remember all mankind is created in the image of God. As mankind does this, tension is reduced, and harmony restored. Make an intentional commitment to let love begin today with you.

Prayer: Father God who created us, we come before you in the name of Jesus offering thanks for the hope you have instilled in us through the blood of Christ Jesus. Help us to live in faith and love, ever striving to become a better example of your new creation in Jesus. Through Christ we pray this. Amen

Day 68

When you are in distress and all these things have
happened to you, then in later days you will return to the
LORD your God and obey him. (Deuteronomy 4:30 NIV)

The world offers many a trophy which to the world indicates success. As we acquire many such trophies they become idols and take the place of God in our lives. People will tend to go to any length to hold onto their prized possession. All the prizes this world has to offer will one day fade, and decay, rust, and disappoint when its value becomes naught. Only God alone will not disappoint. Through Christ Jesus we have victory and will receive the crown of life.

Prayer: Father God, despite the negativity of this world we can look to you as our source of blessing. You O God turn our disappointments around.

Thank you for allowing the disappointments which enable us to appreciate the victories even more. Through Christ our victor we pray. Amen

Day 69

Blessed is the man who finds wisdom, the man who gains understanding. (Proverbs 3:13 NIV)

The Bible teaches that the wisest of all men was Solomon. This helps us understand that wisdom is to be sought after before riches and fame. If a person is wise, then even during lack their wise decisions can promote and sustain life. But the unwise will squander what little resources he has and condemn himself and others to demise. Wisdom provides clarity of thought and accurate action.

Prayer: Father God in Heaven, grant me wisdom above all things. Give to me understanding in those things which confuse and confound. Father God let the words which flow out of my heart offer wise council to all who hear me. In Jesus' name I pray. Amen

Day 70

I am the good shepherd; I know my sheep and my sheep know me. (John 10:14 NIV)

How pleasant it is to have such a personal relationship with the Lord Jesus Christ, that you know his voice as he speaks to you. What is even more wonderful is that he knows your voice when you speak to him. Our Lord leads us as the good Shepherd and we follow in the full knowledge that we are fully protected from all hurt, harm and danger.

Prayer: Lord Jesus you are the great shepherd who leads us his wayward sheep. Through your tender care guide, us in the renewal of emulating you daily and becoming more Christ like in our thoughts, words and deeds. Help us to be rooted in you Lord Jesus. This we pray in the name of the Father, the Son and Holy Spirit. Amen

Day 71

I am the Living One; I was dead, and behold I am alive
forever and ever! And I hold the keys of death and
Hades. (Revelation 1:18 NIV)

Because Jesus lives' we too shall not die in eternity but shall be raised
to life when He comes to claim all who are his. This will be reminiscent
of the Negro Spiritual "When the Saints go marching in". When we
breathe our last on this earth the body we now possess will rest until
the return of Christ. On that day we will be carried to the new city
which will have been prepared for his prepared people.

Prayer: Thank you Father God, for sending your Son Jesus Christ to
defeat the power of death and provide us the ultimate victory and
eternal life. In Jesus' name we pray. Amen

Day 72

The LORD is good, a refuge in times of trouble. He cares
for those who trust in him. (Nahum 1:7 NIV)

Life throws us curves. Those challenges come from friend and stranger
alike. How difficult life can be if you face it alone without the calm
assurance given by knowing the Lord Jesus Christ as your help in times
of trouble. You are his, he cares for you as you go through the storms
of life. Know that you are not alone.

Prayer: Father God, as we live this life we find that we are inundated
with the cares and uncertainties of life. Your word illustrates that you
care for even the smallest creatures on this planet. Help me to walk
in that assurance that you care for me regardless of what this world
throws at me. In Jesus' name we pray. Amen

Day 73

A man's wisdom gives him patience; it is to his glory to overlook an offense. (Proverbs 19:11 NIV)

How often have you encountered people who were short with you, or for that matter you were short with them? We often tend to have little patience with one another; yet we want that same patience exhibited towards us. As we develop the ability to bear with one another we sense serenity as it encompasses us, this then manifests in all our interactions with one another. This brings peace.

Prayer: Father God, we children of men lack patience with one another. Heavenly Father let the irritants of this world not so deeply affect us. Help us to be long suffering with self and one another. In Jesus' name we pray. Amen

Day 74

I consider that our present sufferings are not worth comparing with the glory that will be revealed in us. (Romans 8:18 NIV)

"I can't take it anymore". Have you ever thought that to yourself? People let you down. Situations become burdensome which should be easily solved. It seems as if you cannot live life you must endure life. Take heart! "This too shall pass". This quote speaks to us in life alerting us that this is only temporary. We are passing through this life and not one person will be required to endure in the life to come as the glory of our Savior will be revealed to us. Hold on!

Prayer: Father God of mercy and comfort, we children of men experience from day to day the afflictions of this world. We have strained relationships, persuasion to compromise our morals and standards. Fraud is perpetrated against us. Betrayal of our trust by a confidant brings us much pain. People perpetuate falsehoods about us. Yet the troubles of this world are nothing in comparison to the glory which you have prepared for us at the time Christ will return to carry us home. Thank you for the comfort which abounds through Christ Jesus. In Jesus' name we pray. Amen

Day 75

So, whoever knows the right thing to do and fails to do
it, for him it is sin. (James 4:17 ESV)

How often have you heard the saying, "well it was just a tiny sin"? Or how often have you heard the phrase "I only told a little white lie"? We as carnal people tend to sugar coat out flirtation with sin, thinking we are not being held accountable for such a small infraction of God's law. The truth is if you steal a penny or a million dollars you have committed a sin. The fact is if you see your fellow human beings in an act which is sinful, and you do not attempt to correct them then you and they are sinning. We sin by what we do and what we leave undone. We sin in thought when it is not made obedient to Christ. We also sin in word and deed.

Lord, we sin by commission and Lord we sin by omission. Father God, we are aware that when you know better you should do better, but that is not always the case for your handmade servants. Help us O Lord to do better as we seek to follow your will for our lives. Lord in your mercy, hear our prayer. Forgive us for the sake of the bitter suffering and death of Jesus. Amen

Day 76

For our offenses are many in your sight, and our sins
testify against us. Our offenses are ever with us, and we
acknowledge our iniquities. (Isaiah 59:12 NIV)

If it were not for the forgiveness of sin offered us through the sacrificial blood of the Lamb of God Jesus Christ, we would all be lost. Attempting to evade sin in our lives is like trying to walk through a junkyard of greasy scrap machinery clothed entirely in white. You will not make it through without getting some on you. Isn't it wonderful that we have such a forgiving God? All we need do is approach him in repentance, confessing our sin and he will forgive. He is waiting, come to him.

Prayer: Merciful Father God, thank you for the forgiveness of sin. We try to white wash our sin, yet you continue to forgive if we come to you with repentant hearts. Help your people with un-confessed sin so that we may come before you fully repentant and become wholly clean by your grace. In Jesus' name we pray. Amen

Day 77

> For God so loved the world, that he gave his only
> begotten Son, that whosoever believeth in him should
> not perish, but have everlasting life. (John 3:16 KJV)

The love of God is unparalleled. In our human condition we see the love of parents, particularly the love of a mother. A parent in many cases will go all out for the child born to them. But even the human parent has a limit when love ceases as the definitive emotion especially when children become disobedient, belligerent, defiant or wayward. This demonstrates that mankind loves because of, but God on the other hand loves in spite, of. God is long suffering with his people and went on to give up his only begotten son for a sinful humanity. This he did, regardless of man's sinful action although mankind has an ingrained conscientiousness of right and wrong.

Prayer: Thank you Lord God Almighty for loving us when no one else could or would. Thank you for sacrificing the most precious gift of heaven so we could one day join you where you are. Of all the gifts we've ever received, yours is the best. We offer this praise in the name of Jesus whose gift has given us life. Amen

Day 78

For prophecy never had its origin in the will of man,
but men spoke from God as they were carried along by
the Holy Spirit. (2 Peter 1:21 NIV)

Which way to go? What should I do? These are questions we ask each day as we rise to begin our daily lives. How difficult it is to move when you do not know what to do are where to go. Our guide the Holy Spirit should be our first contact as we pursue our daily activities. Often, we begin our undertaking under the power of self-direction, then as we seem to be traveling through a labyrinth we wonder why. We need to place our guidance in the hands of the trailblazer who knows the beginning from the end of our journey. In doing this we cannot get lost in the hustle and bustle of daily activity.

Prayer: Gracious and Eternal Father God, it is only through your word as the Spirit gives it that we each day find our direction. When we seek direction from our flesh we go astray. Help us to live the life given by your Spirit and shun the path of death given by the flesh. In Jesus' name we pray. Amen

Day 79

then I saw all that God has done. No one can
comprehend what goes on under the sun. Despite
all his efforts to search it out, man cannot discover
its meaning. Even if a wise man claims he knows, he
cannot really comprehend it. (Ecclesiastes 8:17 NIV)

People ask the question, "How can God forgive me this". In life we often make choices which causes us to walk under the umbrella of dread and shame. When you have done something so horrific that in your heart you believe God cannot forgive you then remember that his ways are not your ways, his thoughts are not your thoughts. As God's precious people we must approach him with a repentant and contrite hearts, asking forgiveness for the infraction in question. God desires to forgive and remove your sin from as far as the east is from the west.

Prayer: Heavenly Father, your amazing grace is beyond our limited comprehension. Help us to channel that grace through our lives into the lives of others. In Jesus' name we pray. Amen

Day 80

> None of those condemned things shall be found in your
> hands, so that the Lord will turn from his fierce anger;
> he will show you mercy, have compassion on you, and
> increase your numbers, as he promised on oath to your
> forefathers. (Deuteronomy 13:17 NIV)

God's precious people get so caught up in acting out by allowing themselves to become immersed in worldly activities, which when viewed under the light of God's word resemble idol worship. As God's children we should seek to refrain from placing such a high value on earthly commodities, behavior, icons and anything which causes us to take our focus away from our Lord and Savior Jesus Christ who shed his blood for our redemption. It is the Lord your God you must follow, and him you must revere. Keep his commands and obey him; serve him and hold fast to him.

Prayer: God of love and compassion, forgive us as we often operate in our sinful nature. Help us to reflect love in a manner which emulates you as we seek to reject sinful activity. Help us to exhibit patience with our brothers and sisters in every aspect of interaction with one another, offering only pure love. Through Jesus we ask this. Amen

Day 81

> Let us fix our eyes on Jesus, the author and perfecter
> of our faith, who for the joy set before him endured the

cross, scorning its shame, and sat down at the right
hand of the throne of God. (Hebrews 12:2 NIV)

Without Jesus we would not have life. As it is written he created all
that is, was and ever shall be and nothing that was created was done so
without him. In every aspect of life, our gaze should ever turn towards
Christ Jesus through whom we have our being. Jesus suffered shame
and humiliation on our behalf, therefore each of us should continually
reflect on his sacrificial act which brought us into right relationship
with God the Father.

Prayer: Lord God of Heaven and Earth, when the tough times come
upon us help us to remember that we must look to the man of Calvary,
Jesus the author and finisher of our faith. Embed in our spirits that it
is through Christ Jesus that our courage becomes renewed. In Jesus'
name we pray. Amen

Day 82

He who did not spare his own Son, but gave him up for
us all, how will he not also, along with him, graciously
give us all things? (Romans 8:32 NIV)

Ask yourself, do I deserve what God gives me while I am on this side
of eternity? God in his merciful grace gives us life, love, activities of
our limbs, an unclouded mind, relationships and most of all salvation.
At what cost does all of this come, it took the death of Christ Jesus to
illustrate the full impact of God's Amazing Grace. Who is like God?

Prayer: Dear Father God creator of heaven and earth, thank you for
the grace you so freely give. As we come to better understand your
grace our hearts become filled with gratitude for your undeserved
benevolence. Because of your grace I know that one day I shall see
your goodness in the land of the living. In Jesus' name we pray. Amen

Day 83

We love because he first loved us. (1 John 4:19 NIV)

Love is perhaps the most loosely used word in the English language. People use this word to gain favor with others or to weaken the defenses people have erected to protect themselves from abuse. We all want to be loved it is our deepest desire so when we perceive there is a chance for true love to manifest in our lives we allow ourselves to become vulnerable to the person who proclaim love for us. Only God offers perfect love. Our desire should be to emulate his love for one another. What a wonderful world this would be if love were pure and undefiled.

Prayer: Gracious Father God in heaven, we often give only lip service to allocating love in this world. Only from you does true love emanate because you are love. We children of men place stipulations on our presentation of love and then only superficially. Warm our hearts O God to extend true love one to another. In Jesus' name we pray. Amen

Day 84

for we were born only yesterday and know nothing,
and our days on earth are but a shadow. (Job 8:9 NIV)

God knows about our ending before we have our beginning. He sees every yesterday, today and the next day. As you think of your days on earth those past and those future ask your self are you pleased with how you lived your past days. If you can see opportunity for improvement make your today a day lived for, by and through Christ so those future days will be full of Christian promise.

Prayer: Holy God of all creation, you viewed our yesterdays; you see our today's and know our coming days. Yet you continue to love us regardless of our weakness. We fall short by what we do and what we do not do. Father God bring us to repentance. For the sake of the innocent bitter suffering of our Lord and Savior Jesus Christ forgive us and help us to forgive others. Through Christ Jesus we pray this. Amen

Day 85

> If you, O Lord, kept a record of sins, O Lord, who could stand? (Psalms 130:3 NIV)

Our God and Father is very patient with us. If we were shown out sinful acts during the passage of a single day we would not believe how often we fall short. We sin in thought, word, and deed; by what we do and by what we leave undone. God chooses not to give us what we deserve but only what his mercy dictates. Because of how he treats us it would benefit others for us to treat them likewise.

Prayer: Holy Righteous and Loving God in the name of Jesus I thank you for not keeping a record of our sins. Because of Jesus our sins are far removed from us as we confess him as our Lord and Savior. The blood of Christ Jesus has erased our sin and brought us into relationship with you. For this reason, your grace can now flow through us for all people. In Jesus' name we pray. Amen

Day 86

> If we confess our sins, he is faithful and just and will forgive us our sins and purify us from all unrighteousness. (1 John 1:9 NIV)

Sin is ever with us. Sin follows us from the womb to the tomb. No matter how well versed we are in God's word sin is right there at the doors of our hearts seeking entrance. As we defend against its assault on one front it attacks from another direction. We are in an endless struggle against sin. Our only defense is to confess immediately our sin as soon as committed while asking Christ to strengthen us to not commit the same sin repeatedly.

Prayer: Father God in Heaven as we children of men go about our daily business we sin by thought, word and deed. Teach us to acknowledge our sins so that we may repent of them, be forgiven of them and put them behind us. In Jesus' name we pray. Amen

Day 87

> But with you there is forgiveness; therefore, you are feared. (Psalms 130:4 NIV)

With the blink of an eye God could bring death to anyone or destruction upon any place he chose. With the awesome power of the God of creation overseeing this world of sinful people we children of God Almighty should be aware that it is only by his unmerited mercy and forgiveness that we are not destroyed. Because God does not destroy us we should not want to destroy one another.

Prayer: Holy Lord Almighty God, through you we have unmerited forgiveness. Pattern us into the image of Christ as we are changed from what this world directs to how Christ Jesus orchestrates our lives. Help us through your spirit to live honorable lives which bring you honor and glory. Through Jesus we ask this. Amen

Day 88

> For surely, O Lord, you bless the righteous; you surround them with your favor as with a shield. (Psalm 5:12 NIV)

The God who created all things which exist is the same God who embellishes his favor upon his chosen ones. God places you in situations where there is true love from family, friends and those who meet you soon come to love and cherish you. The favor of God is also that invisible shield which protects and gives, as the world would define it a charmed life. Such it is to receive the favor of God.

Prayer: Loving Father God, we thank you for your continued favor. Thank you for family, friends and most of all Jesus, in whose name we pray. Amen

Day 89

> He who testifies to these things says, "Yes, I am coming soon." Amen. Come, Lord Jesus. (Revelation 22:20 NIV)

Living life on life's terms is not an easy accomplishment. We encounter troubling and trying times which sometimes test our very will to live. God has given us life. The world gives us trouble. One thing we must remember is trouble won't last always. We have a life ahead of us who are in Christ Jesus just waiting for his return. When Christ returns he will carry with him those who he has a place prepared for in the New Jerusalem. We must patiently await our Savior knowing that something better lies ahead.

Prayer: Come quickly Lord Jesus as this world of sin is spinning out of control. There are those here who eagerly await your new heaven and new earth. As we await your return help us to live faithfully for you. This we sincerely ask in the name of the Father, Son and Holy Spirit. Amen

Day 90

> "Men of Galilee, why do you stand looking into heaven? This Jesus, who was taken up from you into heaven, will come in the same way as you saw him go into heaven." (Acts 1:11 ESV)

Jesus is coming back just as he said he would. He will not return hidden from the sight of mankind he will return just as he left the earth 40 days after his resurrection. Jesus will return to gather unto himself those who will receive the reward of righteousness. When Christ returns he will come riding on the clouds of the heavens what a glorious sight that will be for those who have placed their faith in Christ as Savior.

Prayer: Heavenly Father it is comforting to know that you forgive us because of Christ Jesus. Please never remove your mercy from us. Help us to stand faithful until the return of our Lord and savior Jesus Christ, who will return as he left within the clouds. In Jesus' name we pray. Amen

Day 91

For you have been born again, not of perishable seed,
but of imperishable, through the living and enduring
word of God. (1 Peter 1:23 NIV)

Our whole service to God can be wrapped up in three words "Love one another". If we love those who God has placed on this earth, then we are acting in his will for our lives. This does not mean that we can ever repay God for all he has done in the lives of his people, but this is done out of the love we have for him. When we offer our love, means and service to one another we offer it back to God through them. Even when we do this it comes from God through us as he enables us to do so.

Prayer: Father God, continue your grace in us each day as we give our lives as an offering to you. Help us to assist one another as an offering of our love for you. Give us the ability to live fully through and for you, which is our celebration of all you have given us your created people. Through Christ Jesus we pray. Amen

Day 92

Now the Lord is the Spirit; and where the Spirit of the
Lord is, there is liberty. (2 Corinthians 3:17 NKJV)

What wonderful freedom we have as we allow the Spirit of God to direct our lives. The Spirit gives us life. We have received the breath of life which is the Spirit given by God. Through the spirit we learn to rely on Christ as our means of salvation not on works of our hands who results are often self-serving. When we offer works they are often rooted in sin because we have then reduced the work of Christ on the cross to a point of completion with our personal works towards salvation. The spirit of Christ offers us complete liberty.

Prayer: Heavenly father God we children of men constantly live in bondage to our sinful nature. We thank you Most Holy Lord for providing us liberty from sins penalty. We seek your Spirit because where your Spirit is there is liberty. Through Christ Jesus our liberator we pray. Amen

Day 93

> "You shall not covet your neighbor's house. You shall not covet your neighbor's wife, or his manservant or maidservant, his ox or donkey, or anything that belongs to your neighbor." (Exodus 20:17 NIV)

To seek after that which belongs to another person is to say to God the Father, our provider that you have not done enough. God gives to each person as he desires, and he is not incorrect in what he gives. Some people cannot handle more than is given because they would self-destruct. Be satisfied with what you have and be glad for your neighbors for what they have. Each possession is given by God's perfect will for you.

Prayer: Lord God Heavenly Father, we know you see your people as valuable and of considerable worth. Help us to see each other as you see us. Let us not worry over what others have acquired which causes us to covet but be grateful for what you have given us. Lord God guide us to remember you care for each of us and provide for our needs according to your Holy will. In Jesus' name we pray. Amen

Day 94

> [4]There is one body and one Spirit, just as you were called
> to one hope when you were called, [5]one Lord, one faith,
> one baptism; [6]one God and Father of all, who is over all
> and through all and in all. (Ephesians 4:4-6 NIV)

Because men choose to be guided by their self-conceived notions regarding religion, there are many different denominations which identify themselves with the Christian faith. The fact remains that unless the teachings of Jesus Christ are followed as defined by the Bible in its purity. Anything less or anything more is not of God. We can only Serve God the Father by placing our faith in his Son, Jesus The Christ.

Prayer: Heavenly Father forgive us, change us and help us see what is most important in our lives as your disciples. Break down the barriers that keep us separated into different religious groups and help us find unity around the things, and the One, that matter most, Christ Jesus. In Jesus' name we pray. Amen

Day 95

> O Lord, by your hand save me from such men, from
> men of this world whose reward is in this life. You
> still the hunger of those you cherish; their sons have
> plenty, and they store up wealth for their children.
> (Psalm 17:14 NIV)

The world would assimilate you into its ways if you do not resist. God does not want his chosen people to be integrated in to ways of the world. God desires you to be set apart from the behavior which the world exhibits. As God's blessed people we should seek to carry out divinely inspired actions towards one another which create harmony in the body.

Prayer: Merciful and Almighty Father God, there are times when we become indifferent because of the influences of this world. Lord, call us back before we stray off too far so that we may be in the presence of your love which gives us comfort and joy. Through Christ Jesus we pray. Amen

Day 96

> No, the word is very near you; it is in your mouth and in
> your heart, so you may obey it. (Deuteronomy 30:14 NIV)

People die from starvation due to a lack of food which nourishes the human body. People also die spiritually when there is a lack of spiritual nourishment in the absence of God's Word. As we are willing to share our food with a starving individual we ought to be willing to share the word of God with those starving spiritually. Seek those who hunger and feed them with the Word.

Prayer: Almighty and everlasting Creator, we your hand made servants often miss opportunities to offer the bread of life to those who are starving to death from lack of Spiritual nourishment which is the word. Please make us sensitive to the opportunities which become available to connect people to Christ. In Jesus' name we pray. Amen

Day 97

> I am your servant; give me discernment that I may
> understand your statutes. (Psalm 119:125 NIV)

Our judgment in the light of God's wisdom is foolishness. True wisdom comes only from God above. While we are yet on this side of eternity it is our responsibility to pursue God's wisdom as the foundation for our daily living. This we desire so that our judgment is founded on divine wisdom. Wisdom gives us an accurate trajectory.

Prayer: Holy and Righteous Father, please give me wisdom to discern the way of faithfulness and righteousness in all my dealings. I want to be faithful in the small things that matter to the Kingdom and to my holiness, so that I can be entrusted also with those larger things that matter. Please purify my heart and use my gifts and actions to bring you glory. In Jesus' name we pray. Amen

Day 98

> After this I looked and there before me was a great multitude that no one could count, from every nation, tribe, people and language, standing before the throne and in front of the Lamb. They were wearing white robes and were holding palm branches in their hands. (Revelation 7:9 NIV)

All mankind is created in the image of God. All men speak the language of God in whatever dialect they have been immersed in no matter where on earth. When Christ returns to claim all, who are called by his name there will be peoples of every tribe, tongue, ethnic group, and nation. We all shall stand before the throne of God in numbers no one can count. As we are yet on this side of the cross we must embrace those who do not look like or talk like us because God has created each one, we are all his.

Prayer: Almighty and Everlasting God, help your people to grow more towards the vision you have for your church. Enable us to welcome all people and include all who desire to serve and worship you. Help us to appreciate different worship styles and embrace the many faces, backgrounds and languages which are used to enhance your church. Cause us to remember what John said there was a great multitude from every nation and people from every tongue. Show us how to receive and include all who come seeking Christ. In Jesus' name we pray this. Amen

Day 99

All the nations you have made will come and worship
before you, O Lord; they will bring glory to your name.
(Psalm 86:9 NIV)

We have a task before us while the blood is still flowing warm in our
veins. Our task is to bring glory to our Lord and God. We cannot
accomplish this under our own power but through the power of the
Holy Spirit who teaches us all things, we can realize this. Therefore, we
must pray asking for the divine unction of the Holy Spirit as we seek
to carry out that which glorifies God.

Prayer: Holy Lord, in the power of your Holy Spirit help us to do all that
we can to bring you glory. Thank you for the promise that all we do in
your name is not in vain. Amen

Day 100

See, I have engraved you on the palms of my hands;
your walls are ever before me. (Isaiah 49:16 NIV)

God knows you so very intimately that even the hairs of your head
are numbered. In knowing this we can take comfort that God is ever
present watching over our situations. That does not mean we will not
experience the trials of life. It means that we will not face them alone.
God will take care of you, fear not.

Prayer: Gracious father in Heaven, you know the names of each one
of your children whom you have created. Father you have numbered
the very hair of our heads. It is a comfort to know that you know us
so intimately. There is nothing father that we experience that you are
not aware of. Help us to live contented in your promise "that you will
never leave us or forsake us", knowing that you will take care of us in
all situations. In Jesus' name we pray. Amen

Day 101

The thief comes only to steal and kill and destroy; I
have come that they may have life and have it to the
full. (John 10:10 NIV)

God knows our ending before our beginning. Our entire life is laid
before him. His desire is that we live life to its fullest measure. People
often through hardness of heart limit themselves from a full life. If
we nurture within ourselves a malleable heart, we can see the Lord
at work through us thereby enabling us to live a full and fruitful life.
Then as we enter life's end we can look back with remembrance of a
life resembling the one God intended.

Prayer: Holy God our Creator and Father, you know our every need
before we ask. You know what is best for us and will not cause us harm.
You have given us commandments for a better way of living. Soften the
hearts of your people that we may experience life to its fullest as you
intended through all you have for our benefit. Through Christ Jesus
we ask this. Amen

Day 102

⁹But the LORD God called to the man, "Where are
you?" ¹⁰ He answered, "I heard you in the garden,
and I was afraid because I was naked; so, I hid."
(Genesis 3:9-10 NIV)

Is God calling _____your name_____, where are you? In our
brokenness we sin by what we do and what we do not do, or other sin
not clearly defined in scripture. Like Adam we hide because we are
ashamed. We hide by not praying, attending worship service, Bible
Study or fellowshipping with other believers. Jesus knows our struggle.
Therefore, Jesus came and died for us that we would no longer hide
in shame but boldly come forward saying "Lord it is me standing in
the need of you". Even in our brokenness the Lord still loves and cares

for us saying "Come to me all who are burdened". He also says, "I will never leave you or forsake you". Stop hiding, you can approach him in the confidence of his grace because he loves you!

Prayer: Almighty and holy God, without your grace and the gift of salvation, I could not approach you with confidence. Thank you for sending Jesus to redeem me by the shedding of his precious blood. Thank you for his life, his death, his resurrection, his exaltation and his intercession. Help me through your Holy Spirit to keep my eyes on him. Through his holy name I pray. Amen

Day 103

> [16] Be joyful always; [17] pray continually; [18] give thanks in all circumstances, for this is God's will for you in Christ Jesus. (1 Thessalonians 5:16-18 NIV)

Gratitude is vital in our world. When someone does good toward you it is critical that you acknowledge their kindness in your life. Jesus gave thanks for those God the Father had given him, although they were broken, lacking in understanding, failing in total commitment and fearful. You and I ought to give thanks in all situations regardless of how dim the circumstances seem. God is there and in control of the outcome. Give thanks not because of the difficulties but as you go through them because God is ever present in your life.

Prayer: Holy, Gracious, Merciful and Loving Father God. Life tosses many problems at us daily. We suffer sickness, trials, and numerous other difficulties. Through it all we can find comfort in knowing that you alone Lord will deliver those who are yours out of the afflictions of this worlds. For this our hearts are filled with gratitude for your ongoing salvation, now and into eternity. In Jesus' name I pray. Amen

Day 104

Therefore, if anyone is in Christ, he is a new creation;
old things have passed away; behold, all things have
become new. (2 Corinthians 5:17 NIV)

There seems to be a consensus held by many that they have done so much wrong God has turned his back on them and they must get their lives together before coming into his church. Nothing can be further from the truth. God's work is redemption and restoration of his creation which includes mankind through Christ Jesus. If a person would come to Christ Jesus their redemption is assured. The old things are put away and he becomes a new creation in Jesus. The easiest way for this process to begin is to come forward and hear the word which begins to work faith in the broken heart creating faith.

Prayer: Lord of Hosts, you look at us in a manner which sees not the wounded, scarred sinful disgruntled wretches we are. You, Lord Jesus see us as a new creation which has been prepared through your cleansing blood. Because of the love you have for us you make us special. Thank you for the transformation from detestable to lovable. Thank you for saving us from sin, self and eternal condemnation. Thank you, Lord Jesus. Amen

Day 105

Once you were alienated from God and were
enemies in your minds because of your evil behavior.
(Colossians 1:21NIV)

Do you remember how you once acted in the world? You lied, stole, cheated, deceived and caroused living a life contrary to the teachings of Christ. Then somebody told you or reminded you about Jesus. The Holy Spirit of God convicted you, so you would understand that you could no longer live as enemies of God by embracing sinful worldly ways. You invited the Spirit of God to dwell with you as you sought to change your life to reflect the light of Christ. Through the power of the

Blood of Jesus and the direction of the Holy Spirit you now embrace God's word as the beacon which guides your life.

Prayer: Thank you, Father, for your anguish and cost to forgive my sins by the blood of your Son. I refuse to take lightly the cost of my sin and will live for your glory in appreciation of your grace. In the name of Jesus, the one who sacrificed all for my salvation I pray. Amen

Day 106

> For I know the plans I have for you, declares the Lord,
> plans to prosper you and not to harm you, plans to give
> you hope and a future. (Jeremiah 29:11 NIV)

How does life look to you right now? Are there challenges which seem insurmountable? Does the appearance of all around indicate you are in a vacuum? Despite the appearances; challenges and your personal perception God has not abandoned you. The Lord is the source of prosperity and all that is good. He has good awaiting you. Do not abort your hope in the Lord. He operates in his time not our time he is never late and always on time.

Prayer: Most High Father God, as we approach the future with all its uncertainty we can take comfort in knowing that you are there awaiting our arrival. As we place our trust in you we can confidently approach the future without hesitation because although we do not know what the future holds we know who holds the future. Thank you for being with us always. In Jesus' name I pray. Amen

Day 107

> as far as the east is from the west, so far has he removed
> our transgressions from us. (Psalm 103:12 NIV)

We can do many things for ourselves but there are some things we cannot do for ourselves. One thing you cannot do is stick your elbow into your ear. That may sound amusing to some but none the less it is true. Another thing you cannot do is rid yourselves of the contravention of Almighty God's decrees where sin is concerned. God does for us what we cannot do for ourselves through the precious blood of Jesus. Because of the shed blood of Jesus our sins are removed from us as we place our faith in his redeeming act which occurred upon Calvary's cross. Christ Jesus died that sins penalty would be paid on our behalf. Therefore, we can come to him and confess our sins and forgiveness is given and sin removed

Prayer: God of compassion and forgiveness, forgive our unintentional blasphemy against you. There are times Father when we in our own sufficiency proudly stand before men and proclaim, "I am not a saint". We say this not to give you glory but to deify self in the eyes of others. Work in our hearts a true repentance that the pride of life and the self-interests be far removed. Help us to be that new creation which brings glory to your name through Christ Jesus our Lord. We pray this in the name of Jesus. Amen

Day 108

The Lord will guide you always; he will satisfy your needs in a sun-scorched land and will strengthen your frame. You will be like a well-watered garden, like a spring whose waters never fail. (Isaiah 58:11 NIV)

What's wrong with you? Do all the paths you have chosen in life seem obscure; lifeless and choking? Is it that you cannot seem to find the bright path out of the gloom this world casts all around? Call out to Jesus he knows the way, he is the way. Jesus can carry you through the perplexities of this world because he has overcome the world. Jesus is there to refresh you in this arid and parched land he is that cooling water which quenches the thirst of mankind for eternity. Human flesh cannot guide you, don't rely on it. Rely on Jesus to guide you out from the darkness.

Prayer: Thank you redeeming Savior my Lord Jesus for the living water you so freely give. You say come to you and freely take of the water of life. Only because of the love you have for the inhabitants of this sin filled world do you invite the unrepentant, unloving, self-centered and egotistical to come and be filled. You seek no payment for this life-giving water and yet many reject your free offering to come and refresh their lives that they may blossom into a beautiful fragrant treasure which all mankind will have the opportunity to enjoy and benefit from. Amen

Day 109

> For the earth is the Lord's, and the fullness thereof.
> (1 Corinthians 10:26 KJV)

The Bible is clear that God the Father through Jesus Christ created all things on earth and in heaven. Since all things are created by him all things belong to him. This includes all that dwells on the earth in the seas and under the earth. Even the very breath we breathe comes from our God. God gives us food from both plant and animal. God gives us joy from his realm in heaven and those we encounter here on this earth. All good things come from our God who loves us with an unquenchable love that endures forever.

Prayer: Our father in Heaven. Thank you for our daily provision of life, joy, health, sustenance and your gracious care. You provide for our every need. Help us to understand that the earth is yours and its fullness. You offer to us who inhabit this earth all it possesses as your loving gift to us. In Jesus' name we pray. Amen

Day 110

> I have hidden your word in my heart that I might not
> sin against you. (Psalm 119:11 NIV)

The word of God guides us in our thoughts, words and deeds if we allow it to be the compass which we use to navigate through each circumstance of life.

Prayer: Lord God Almighty and Everlasting, there is none other like you in your majesty and wonder. You Holy Father create, and you obliterate. You give life and you take life. You redeem the fallen and offer salvation to the lost. Thank you for considering us in your ultimate plan for your creation. Give us the ability to follow your perfect will so that we may glorify you in everything we say, think and do. In Jesus' name we pray. Amen

Day 111

> I must work the works of Him who sent Me while it
> is day; the night is coming when no one can work.
> (John 9:4 NKJV)

In our lives we can view life as day and death as night. We have such a short time on this earth to accomplish the work God in Christ has called us to do. If we live for 100 years, that equals 36,525 days of life. Most of mankind will not see 100 years so the time is short. While we have the light of life in our eyes let us seek daily to join God in his work. Night is rapidly approaching when no one can work.

Prayer: Help us Lord Jesus by your name to do the works of him who sent you. Help us to understand and be led by the light of your Holy Word. Amen

Day 112

> Remember this: Whoever sows sparingly will also reap
> sparingly, and whoever sows generously will also reap
> generously. (2 Corinthians 9:6 NIV)

During Biblical times people were farmers and herdsmen. The Bible uses many farming terms to share God's message to His people. Sowing was a means of planting where the farmer would cast hands full of seed to the ground plentifully, with the hopes of a bountiful harvest when it was time to gather what was planted. The more seed was planted the greater the harvest. God teaches us this truth in the giving of our offerings to aid in the work of the Kingdom. God says sow into the kingdom of your time, talents and treasure and watch as He provide you a plentiful harvest. This giving is to be done cheerfully and without reluctance or a feeling of compulsion. Sow into God's inspired ministries so that God's work on earth can be accomplished.

Prayer: Holy Father God as we seek so diligently after the wealth of this world, help us to seek you with equal zeal. Father help us to remember that we ought to store up treasure that will not rust and decay. Show us Father that our passion should be for the things that money cannot buy. Father God help us to give back what you have so generously given us. In Jesus' name I pray. Amen

Day 113

> I am the vine; you are the branches. If a man remains
> in me and I in him, he will bear much fruit; apart from
> me you can do nothing. (John 15:5 NIV)

People want to be self-sufficient. In fact, we deceive ourselves into the misconception that we operate under the power of self will. For us to be productive we must maintain our connection to our Lord Jesus Christ. That vertical connection enables us to function effectively on a horizontal level for the benefit of our families, friends, acquaintances, and our selves. With Christ we can do all things. Without Christ we can do nothing.

Prayer: God of strength, we children of men often attempt to act out of sufficiency of self. As we operate in our own strength we find that we are inadequate to meet the challenges of life. Yet we struggle hopelessly against the vicissitudes of life, not knowing which direction to take because we are lost in our own ineptness because we think, we possess potency to prevail. You are the strength of men help us to grasp that concept that we might experience a more fulfilling life. Through Christ Jesus I pray. Amen

Day 114

> For we must all appear before the judgment seat of
> Christ, that each one may receive what is due him for
> the things done while in the body, whether good or
> bad. (2 Corinthians 5:10 NIV)

The day is coming when we will all stand to be judged for the fruit of our lives. This judgment has nothing to do with your faith in Christ Jesus as our redeeming Savior in whom you have placed your faith. This judgment will be for what you did in life, the good, the bad and the ugly. We, each one is responsible for every thought, word and deed committed while in the body. We will have to answer for the lies, cheating, stealing, bias, infidelity of thought and deed in our personal lives and in our worship of God. We will be called into account for our lack of adherence to God's directives by not pointing the lost to Christ Jesus for salvation. Make subject to the Word of God every thought, word and deed in life so when you stand before the throne you hear the words "Well done my good and faithful servant, well done". What is past being past you cannot correct that but today is a new day for new beginnings. Ask the Savior to help, strengthen and keep you, he will carry you through the rough times.

Prayer: Heavenly Father, there are times in our lives when we lack the understanding or the resolve to follow your word. At those times of spiritual lack gently guide us back onto the path of righteousness. Thank you for Christ Jesus' redemptive power working in our lives. In Jesus' Holy and Precious name, I pray. Amen

Day 115

> (John 6:68 NIV) Simon Peter answered him, "Lord, to
> whom shall we go? You have the words of eternal life.

Life in this world entices us to follow a plethora of people with rubrics of self-enlightened spirituality. People follow human beings who share a gospel message that is little more than a motivational message sprinkled with Biblical Gospel text which makes the uninformed believe this is God's message to them. Often, they teach prosperity and a God who is moved by "quid pro quo". Jesus came asking nothing from us but offering everything to us.

Prayer: Heavenly Father God, in life we scramble after the toys this world has to offer. We want the houses, cars, money and recognition this world has to offer. Lord we even turn to other people as our benefactors and liberators. Father we turn to these things and in doing this we turn away from you. Help us to keep our feet firmly planted in the Gospel of Christ Jesus. We, like Peter desire to say: "Lord, to whom shall we go? You have the words of eternal life". In Jesus' name we pray. Amen

Day 116

> He will wipe away every tear from their eyes, and death
> shall be no more, neither shall there be mourning nor
> crying nor pain anymore, for the former things have
> passed away. (Revelation 21:4 ESV)

Irrespective of the way the world and this life treats us there is joy in the good things which the Lord has done. As Jesus has redeemed us we should always be joyful for this because it leads to the eternal life that we will one day share in his glorious eternal city. Rejoice, good things are coming. You are only passing through this veil of tears. Trouble won't last always.

Prayer: Heavenly Father God we approach you in the name of Jesus thanking you for life. Father we live in this veil of tears called earth which gives each of us more than our share of troubles. There are situations which bring us to tears. There is loss of relationships which bring us to tears. There is the loss of loved ones which bring us to tears. Father God we look forward to the day when you will wipe away every tear from the eyes of your people. Merciful Comforter we await the day of no more mourning. Heavenly Father, thank you for the promise found in Christ Jesus which will allow the former things to pass away. In Jesus' name we pray. Amen

Day 117

> Wait for the Lord; be strong and let your heart take
> courage; wait for the Lord! (Psalm 27:14 ESV)

Sin is ever knocking at our door. Satan devises schemes geared to peak our interest because of the desires of our hearts. He knows what best entices you; that is what he lures you with. Fight sin, tooth and nail, bite, claw, punch and kick to defend yourself stand behind the word of God. Unfortunately sin always has its way with us in one form or another so we cannot escape it in this life. Be encouraged, we have an advocate who speaks for us. Jesus comes to our rescue defending us and stands between Satan's accusations and ushers in God Grace on our behalf. Shun evil and sin in every form. Call on Jesus to protect and defend you, he will if you ask him.

Prayer: Almighty and Everlasting Father God, forgive us our trespasses. Thank you for the goodness you promised us even in the brokenness of our sinful nature. Thank you for the sacrifice of Jesus who died so that our sins would be forgiven. We wait on you Lord; help our hearts to be courageous. In Jesus' name we pray. Amen

Day 118

> Behold, I am with you and will keep you wherever you
> go and will bring you back to this land. For I will not
> leave you until I have done what I have promised you.
> (Genesis 28:15 ESV)

To the Biblical patriarchs God spoke words which assured them he was always near. God speaks into the lives of those who are of the household of faith. To the faithful God is ever saying I am with you in all circumstances. I have promised to never leave or forsake those who are mine; of this you can be confident.

Prayer: Holy and Faithful God of creation, we praise you that you are ever with us in our jaunt through life. Thank you, Father God for keeping us wherever we go and in every circumstance. You are there Lord even when we cannot perceive your presence, watching over your precious children. Thank you that through Christ Jesus we will not be lost. Hear O God our voices of gratitude. In Jesus' name we pray. Amen

Day 119

> And Jabez called on the God of Israel saying, "Oh, that You would bless me indeed, and enlarge my territory, that Your hand would be with me, and that You would keep me from evil, that I may not cause pain!" So, God granted him what he requested. (1 Chronicles 4:10 NKJV)

As Jabez prayed that any possible disaster that might be initiated by him be turned into a blessing we also have the listening ear of our God. It is only through the power of our loving God that the liabilities of the human nature can be overcome. Go to God in prayer asking for blessing, character and protection. He is willing and able to provide each of our desires and needs.

Prayer: O God our Father in Heaven we approach you in the name of Jesus. We ask that you bless us that we may be a blessing to others. Please Lord expand our realm of influence and sojourn with us in this place. Protect us Lord God almighty from the evil one and all of his demonic manipulations. Help us to not cause pain to others but to assist and encourage. In Jesus' name we pray. Amen

Day 120

If we confess our sins, he is faithful and just to forgive
us our sins and to cleanse us from all unrighteousness.
(1 John 1:9 NKJV)

Sin is everywhere; we cannot escape it. As we go about our daily
business sin is crouching like a tiger ready to spring from the recesses
of darkness to subdue, entangle and consume you. As you first become
conscious of sin's manifestation in your life, cast the light of conscious
confession upon it which dilutes its hold and power over you. Ask the
Lord that you not repeat that sin again, saying "Lord deliver me from
evil".

Prayer: Gracious and Merciful God in Heaven, forgive us for attempting
to minimize our sins. We know to do what is right yet we do not do
what is right. Please forgive our sins of commission and our sins of
omission. Father God place our feet on solid ground that we may not
sink in the mire of our iniquity. Father God hear our cry for the sake
of Jesus' bitter suffering and death. In Jesus name we ask this. Amen

Day 121

"I will not leave you as orphans; I will come to you.
(John 14:18 NKJV)

Jesus says to us his people that we are not being abandoned. The
day is rapidly approaching and is closer today than it was yesterday
when we will again see Jesus standing among his people. While not
with us physically now, the spirit of Christ indwells us and is ever
residing with us in this life. We do not need to deal with the pangs of
loneliness because Jesus is with us in spirit now and will return one
day embodied.

Prayer: Thank you Lord Jesus for not abandoning us as those who have
no one to call on. We wait eagerly for your return. You have said "I will

come to you". Come Lord Jesus come. This we pray in the name of the Father, Son and Holy Spirit. Amen

Day 122

> The blood shall be a sign for you, on the houses where you are. And when I see the blood, I will pass over you, and no plague will befall you to destroy you, when I strike the land of Egypt. (Exodus 12:13 ESV)

It is under the blood that we see The Lord God's miraculous mercy affecting our lives in a positive manner. When the world around us is experiencing the negativity of its actions we experience the peace; share in grace and know without a doubt God's Amazing Grace. It's the blood of Jesus that will never lose its power.

Prayer: O Lord our God, Maker of Heaven and Earth. We justly deserve your present and eternal punishment for the sin which dominates our lives. Father God, thank you for sending our propitiation Jesus, the precious Lamb of God who takes away the sins of the world. Thank you, Father God for seeing the blood of the unblemished lamb smeared on the doorposts of our lives and you pass over by not imposing the judgment of eternal death. Thank you, Lord for offering us a means of conciliation through Christ Jesus, our Lord and savior. In Jesus' name we pray. Amen

Day 123

> And he brought us out from there, that he might bring us in and give us the land that he swore to give to our fathers. (Deuteronomy 6:23 ESV)

Our loving and redeeming Father God has brought us out of the bondage of sin with its conviction of eternal death into the freedom of reconciliation which Christ Jesus provides for us by offering eternal life.

Prayer: Lord God Almighty, Awesome and full of grace. You have allowed your grace to abound in the lives of your people. You are the God who brought us out of sin that we may be brought into your presence. Thank you for being glorious, compassionate, merciful and caring. Thank you for Christ Jesus who is the embodiment of each of these attributes. In Jesus' name we pray. Amen

Day 124

> Now may the God of peace himself sanctify you completely and may your whole spirit and soul and body be kept blameless at the coming of our Lord Jesus Christ. (1 Thessalonians 5:23 ESV)

We serve a triune God one God three persons, Father, Son and Holy Spirit "The Trinity". God has made man in his image and likewise has given man three distinct parts which combine into the one person. God has given us the breath of life (Spirit), this he placed within human flesh (Body) and given us free will through thought (Soul/Mind). As God's created people we are to use this life which is enveloped in Spirit, body and soul to serve and worship our creator God and to live in harmony with one another. Seek your help from our loving God to help you live as he desires for mankind until the day Christ Jesus returns to carry us home to the New Jerusalem. Through him you can do it!

Prayer: Lord God Almighty, you are mighty in power, compassionate in grace and full of love and peace. Thank you for continued blessings. Help us to remain blameless in mind, body and spirit until the return of our Lord and Savior Jesus Christ. In Jesus' name we pray. Amen

Day 125

> To everything there is a season, and a time to every purpose under the heaven. (Ecclesiastes 3:1 KJV)

We cannot safely proceed forward looking backwards. You know where you have been, but you do not know what is up ahead. Human life is filled with time and change. You as an individual cannot control the times or changes of life. Just know that for those who are in Christ Jesus the times and changes are predestined and all will work for the good of those who love the Lord. You can feel secure of your future when Christ is there awaiting you in your future.

Prayer: Most Holy, Almighty, Loving and Gracious God. We children of men go through life attempting to live life while looking back at past accomplishments. Give us Father God the Spirit of rebirth and refreshment that we can allow past seasons to remain in the past as memories which bring joy, not as the solitary building block for our now time experiences. Help us to seek your face as we march forward towards eternity, walking in your divine guidance and grace. Lord lead us and guide us along our way. This we ask in Jesus' precious name. Amen

Day 126

Let love be genuine. Abhor what is evil; hold fast to
what is good. (Romans 12:9 ESV)

For people when they want something from another and are seeking the path of least resistance the words "I love you" easily roll from the tongue. It is deceptive to falsely use this endearing term for selfish gain. Our creator God is love and to use love as a means of obtaining our desire is demeaning the very nature of God. Love must be pure and undefiled. It is evil to lie about something as sacred as love.

Prayer: Father God in Heaven, there are times when we allow sin to come into our lives because we have become desensitized to it. Heavenly Father God we tolerate that which is evil by saying to ourselves we have Christian freedom and we are demonstrating enlightenment and sophistication. Holy Lord quicken our spirits to reject what is evil and embrace what is good, pure and of divine origin. Father God hear our prayer, we ask in the name of Jesus our Lord and savior. Amen

Day 127

> Blessed is the man who walks not in the counsel of the wicked, nor stands in the way of sinners, nor sits in the seat of scoffers. (Psalm 1:1 ESV)

Those who revere the Lord seek to avoid immoral guidance and activity. Ungodly ways are a vexation to the spirit of the person who knows God is vital to and head of their life. The blessed always seem to be in a perpetual state of happiness. The wicked are always in turmoil. Avoid those who mock God and ridicule his word and reject his law, their end is the second death.

Prayer: Blessed Lord our Father and Our God, give us a discerning spirit to know and understand the modality of those we encounter daily. Guide us that we not be infected by the evil influences which guide some of the people of this earth but let us rather influence them by our display of character which is led by the Gospel of Jesus Christ. Help us to lead people down the narrow path which leads to salvation. In Jesus name we ask this. Amen

Day 128

> But God chose what is foolish in the world to shame the wise; God chose what is weak in the world to shame the strong. (1 Corinthians 1:27 NIV)

In the world in which we live we think of the licentious, prostitutes, alcoholics, murders, liars, addicted and thieves as undesirable people who we choose not to associate with or even be acknowledged as being known by them. However, these are the kinds of people God used, those people and those things which in our natural minds are the irrational people and things of the world. The God of creation can use the illogical people, places and things to accomplish his kingdom building process. What seems idiotic, imprudent, silly and unwise is what God uses to confound the enemy and those who are not sensitive to his Holy Spirit's calling who is issuing them a call to participate in what he is doing. Of all the irrational things God has done and continues to do, he died an ignominious death on a cross to save those who were his enemies and not called by his name.

Prayer: Our Father in Heaven, you have chosen what the world perceives as foolish and through that you shame the wise. The world says, "why would God give up his riches in Heaven and come to dwell among his creation"? The world thinks this is foolish. But Father your word says even the cross upon which salvation was won is foolishness to those who are perishing. To the world O God, it looks weak to turn the other cheek to those who would do us harm. But God Our LORD you use the weak things of the world to shame the strong. Thank you for allowing us to be a part of your kingdom building process. In Jesus name we pray. Amen

Day 129

> And the Lord will guide you continually and satisfy your
> desire in scorched places and make your bones strong;
> and you shall be like a watered garden, like a spring
> of water, whose waters do not fail. (Isaiah 58:11 ESV)

Nothing grows in an arid and scorched land. So too nothing useful comes out of the dry person who walks through life barren of the life-giving water of God's divine word. If you believe in Christ Jesus, he said streams of living water shall pour forth from you. You will be vigorous as a living testimony of God's abundant blessings.

Prayer: Heavenly Father God, your children sometimes find themselves in scorched arid places. In those dry places we find ourselves without refreshment. Thank you, Father God for the living water of your Word which comforts us despite the refreshment which is being withheld by those who have opportunity to share the living water through the word. Thank you for guiding us continually although it is a parched land we find ourselves dwelling in. Thank you, Lord that through Christ Jesus you make our bones strong and we then become like a watered garden in the middle of drought. Thank you, Father in the name of Jesus Christ our living water. Amen

Day 130

If you abide in me, and my words abide in you, ask whatever you wish, and it will be done for you. (John 15:7 ESV)

We approach the Lord our God through the medium of communication we know as prayer. This is serious business, talking to God. Before we approach God to speak to him we must first know who he is. It is impossible to talk to him apart from knowing and believing his teachings. Jesus says to ask whatever we will in his name so that he may bring glory to the Father. Our prayers must carry forward the work of Christ Jesus. The work of Jesus is to save that which is lost. So, our prayers should emulate that effort as we direct people to Christ as their savior. Our prayer then also should be to ask the best for everyone, those whom we love and those not so loved. Our prayer should request a renewed love for all of God's precious people.

Prayer: Lord God almighty Creator of Heaven and Earth, we praise you that you allow us to remain in you through a relationship which is initiated by and through you. We all fall short of your glory, yet you never turn away. Thank you that through your word we can approach you with hope because exposure to that word leaves a vestige of it implanted in our spirits. Your word says to ask what we will; we ask to be more Christ like so that this world might be a better place for us all. In Jesus' name we pray. Amen

Day 131

"Yet even now," declares the Lord, "return to me with
all your heart, with fasting, with weeping, and with
mourning. (Joel 2:12 ESV)

The Lord God is ever awaiting the return of any of his broken children.
Our nature makes us sinful; it is an inherited trait common to all
mankind. The Lord allows us the opportunity to return to him even
after our failures because of his unfailing mercy and grace. Approach
the Lord with a repentant heart; confess your failure and he will forgive
and restore you. This he does without hesitation.

Prayer: Heavenly Father God our Jehovah-Rohi. We your hand made
servants like little lost sheep constantly go astray. We stray and do not
listen as we are called by your word to atone. Yet with compassion you
call us to return to you. You turn a blind eye and accept us just as we
are. Who is there like you giving another chance repeatedly to those
who continually turn away? Thank you for your grace, mercy and
unconditional love which were demonstrated through Jesus Christ.
Instill in us the ability and desire necessary to seek your forgiveness.
In Jesus' name we pray. Amen

Day 132

and rend your hearts and not your garments." Return
to the Lord, your God, for he is gracious and merciful,
slow to anger, and abounding in steadfast love; and he
relents over disaster. (Joel 2:13 ESV)

As small children we learn the difference between right and wrong.
Some of those lessons are hard taught, through spankings, scolding's
and self-inflicted pain as in the case of being told hot, do not touch. Yet
we do it anyway. As we grew older the word of God was taught to us and
through that word we learned of God's commandments for our lives. In
learning of those commandments, we then were made to realize that we

sin. Before we were made aware of sinful activities we were blameless in our own sight but once made aware of sin we found ourselves utterly immersed in sin. We stand guilty before an awesome God because of our sinful nature, yet he offers forgiveness through Christ Jesus.

Prayer: Father God in Heaven we stand before you in shame for our sinful activities. Father we rip away the darkness of our hearts, yet it continually returns. Thank you, Lord for being gracious, merciful slow to anger and abounding in love. Father through the power of your Holy Spirit and the blood of Christ help us to return to you as you intended, pure and unblemished. In the name of Jesus, we ask this. Amen

Day 133

> Let us test and examine our ways and return to the Lord! (Lamentations 3:40 ESV)

We often think of ourselves or other individuals as good people. But upon deeper examination we find that even in our best efforts we are selfish, self-centered and not so good. We sin in thought, word and deed so, we all fail the goodness test. The best we can hope for is that we can arrest our misdeeds in midstream when they manifest themselves in our lives. This we can accomplish by calling our thoughts and actions into submission under and by the name of Jesus.

Prayer: O Lord God El Shaddai, our ways are not your ways and our thoughts are not your thoughts and certainly our actions are often out of alignment with your desire for our lives. We see how we fall short Lord, but we find in our best efforts to correct our faults we cannot get this process right. Help us Father God to walk in your ways as we walk towards eternity. For the sake of the bitter suffering and death of our Lord Jesus Christ help us to be better. We have no one else to call on. In Jesus' name we pray. Amen

Day 134

And Isaac breathed his last, and he died and was gathered to his people, old and full of days. And his sons Esau and Jacob buried him. (Genesis 35:29 ESV)

We all have an appointment that is without the benefit of cancellation. That appointment is death. Because of sin, we are all destined to die. It was sin that brought death into God's perfect creation. The remains of the human body are handled in various ways after death. There is cremation and burial in the earth or at sea which is typical in the Christian community. In other pagan religions there is mummification and other means of handling of the dead bodies. We thank God that at the end of this world Christ will return to claim his people and gather them together for all of eternity.

Prayer: Gracious Father God thank you for the assurance that on the last day of this world as we know it Our Lord and Savior Jesus Christ will return to carry us home with him. Thank you that we will be gathered with our people and with all people who are yours. Thank you for this blessed assurance which comes because of Christ Jesus, "the Lamb of God who takes away the sins of the world". In Jesus' name we pray. Amen

Day 135

Fear not, for I am with you; I will bring your offspring from the east, and from the west I will gather you. (Isaiah 43:5 ESV)

In your respective lives' you must bear burdens which seem insurmountable. It is at those times when you seem all alone that you feel like God is somewhere sleeping. It is at those times when you feel like you could just curl up in a corner some place in the fetal position because there seems no relief from your situation; it has in your mind become untenable and you feel helpless. Trouble does not discriminate it crosses ethnic, gender, economic, religious, social and moral boundaries. Bad things happen to us all. It is time for you to stop struggling against the current. It is at these times we turn back to God's word where we find relief.

Prayer: Holy Father God in Heaven, as we your handmade servants go through life we are tossed and driven by many trials and much trouble. Father we would like to have the calm sunny days, but we often find our days overcast with tumultuous storm clouds which pour down a deluge of difficulty. Lord no matter how dark the days look to us, imprint in our Spirits that nothing can separate us from you. Help us to know that we are under your watchful eye and we should fear not. Thank you, Lord Jesus, for overcoming the world; that through you we too are victorious. In Jesus' name we pray. Amen

Day 136

> Behold, I have refined you, but not as silver; I have tried
> you in the furnace of affliction. (Isaiah 48:10 ESV)

Sometimes it takes pain for us to realize there is a different mode or method we must follow. Hardship is never easy to endure but as we endure the difficulties of life we are being made stronger. What does not kill you makes you stronger. This is the reason behind vaccinations. How can we know good times if we do not experience difficult times? Trying times are troubling times when faith in the Lord is the only certain foundation upon which we can find comfort. Ask the lord to walk with you through the troubles and when you come through you will be a better person.

Prayer: Holy Lord God Almighty, there are many times in life when we are immersed in the difficulties associated with living in this broken world. Thank you, Lord for guiding us through those refining trials which change us for the better. We praise you Lord God that when we have come through we have been refined and the dross is removed. It is then that we shine forth as the wholesome people of God who began to resemble our Lord and Savior Jesus Christ who came to this world pure and undefiled. In Jesus' name we pray. Amen

Day 137

¹⁵Love not the world, neither the things that are in the world. If any man loves the world, the love of the Father is not in him. ¹⁶For all that is in the world, the lust of the flesh, and the lust of the eyes, and the pride of life, is not of the Father, but is of the world. (1 John 2:15-16 KJV)

This world has a multitude of enticements to lure us into following its beckoning call towards what it has to offer. The things of this world will all one day pass away. The day will come when there will be no more cars, clothes, and diamond rings. The things we value now will then have no value but be regarded as trash. Only what God has established through Christ will last into eternity. We are but pilgrims passing through this world; we should not allow the trappings of the world seduce us into forgetting where our true home is with Jesus.

Prayer: Father God, Creator of Heaven and Earth there are many temptations set out before your children in this world. Strengthen us to look to you and not that thing which give only temporary comfort to our body, eyes and egos. Holy Lord, help us to subdue the lust of the flesh. Precious Lord turn our head away from that which our eyes seek which is not born of your Heavenly Kingdom. Lord of Mercy remove any fiber of arrogance that is found in our being. Father all this we ask in Jesus' name. Amen

Day 138

"Son of man, these men have taken their idols into their hearts, and set the stumbling block of their iniquity before their faces. Should I indeed let myself be consulted by them? (Ezekiel 14:3 ESV)

The Lord God Almighty has given as his first command that we should have no other gods before him. Even our own self-importance is an idol of which we God's handmade children often use as an attempt to usurp the authority of our creator God. The Lord God will not act on our behalf is we act as gods unto ourselves. As people in this world we easily find ourselves in the grip of worldly assets, prosperity or statuses which we idolize. Help us Lord through the power of the cross to turn away from worldly idols and return to Christ Jesus as our focus of worship.

Prayer: Almighty and Everlasting God our Father who created all that was is and ever shall be we ask that you hear our prayer in the name of Jesus. Father God we children of men embrace many things in this world which we perceive will offer fulfillment of a need. Yet upon obtaining them we find that the promise of fulfillment still leaves us empty and in want. Lord we crave in our hearts hungrily after the effluvial items this world has to offer which offer no satisfaction. Father God break the stronghold of idolatry and its cravings in our hearts. Heavenly Father teach our hearts to worship you. Hear our prayer in Jesus' name. Amen

Day 139

He guards the paths of justice and preserves the way
of His saints. (Proverbs 2:8 NKJV)

Was it fair that Christ Jesus stood in for our sin and received the punishment we so justly deserve? In our heart we know we are due an extreme punishment for our lack of love and sinful errors. Thank God he took upon himself our warranted punishment. The God we serve gives justice to his people despite their failures and shortcomings. God sustains us, protects us, safeguards us because we are his simultaneously saint and sinner creation.

Prayer: Lord God our Protector, our path through life is scattered with obstacles which hinder and sometimes cause damage. Lord as we place our trust in you we find that the rough places have become smooth and the dangers have been canceled. Thank you, Lord God Almighty through Our Lord and savior Jesus Christ that you have safeguarded our pathway as only you can. In Jesus' name we pray Amen

Day 141

So, Abraham called the name of that place, "The Lord will provide"; as it is said to this day, "On the mount of the Lord it shall be provided." (Genesis 22:14 ESV)

God will provide or Jehovah-jireh is the name of the place where Abraham carried Isaac to be sacrificed. God is our provider of the sustenance we need in this life. Our sustenance consists of spiritual food for our souls and nutritional food for our bodies.

Prayer: Lord God of provision, you freely give to your created servants all that is needed to sustain life. Thank you for food, shelter, clothing, goods, assets and love. Thank you most of all for the love demonstrated through Christ Jesus who died that we might be redeemed of the separation from you sin brought into this world. In the precious name of Jesus, we pray. Amen

Day 142

I will greatly rejoice in the Lord; my soul shall exult in my God, for he has clothed me with the garments of salvation; he has covered me with the robe of righteousness, as a bridegroom decks himself like a priest with a beautiful headdress, and as a bride adorns herself with her jewels. (Isaiah 61:10 ESV)

If we take the time to recall all that the Lord has completed in our lives, we can't help rejoicing over his abundant favor and blessings. The greatest of his works is that he called us into relationship with

Christ Jesus who is the author of our salvation. We were walking in a world of darkness immersed in our sinful nature headed to hell without recourse but then Jesus came into our lives as our saving redeemer. As we placed our faith in Jesus we were then clothed in righteousness in the Father's sight. How can we not delight and rejoice in the transforming work of the Lord which has covered us?

Prayer: Lord of Salvation we glory in the triumph you have accomplished on our behalf. We thank you for the garments of salvation which are found in your precious blood which washes us clean and clothes us before the eyes of our Father the Lord God Almighty. In you alone is salvation found and we offer up hearts of gratitude for your shed blood of redemption which saved us from a burning hell. Thank you, Lord Jesus. Amen

Day 143

> I am not ashamed of the gospel, because it is the power
> of God for the salvation of everyone who believes: first
> for the Jew, then for the Gentile. (Romans 1:16 NIV)

To be ashamed of the gospel is to reject life. The Good news of salvation found in the sacrifice of Jesus is something to be embraced by all mankind. Jesus died for every man, woman, boy and girl. Because we know and understand the beauty and significance of this good news, we should want to share the message of salvation with everyone with whom we encounter. We should boldly proclaim what Jesus has done on our behalf to offer us eternal life with him after life on this earth.

Prayer: Father God in Heaven, your word is good news to our ears in this world where there is so much discord and confusion. Help us to shamelessly share the Good News with those of the world who do not know Christ as their Lord and Savior. Speak through us that salvation comes by no other name but that of Jesus. Send us Lord God across religious boundaries to boldly share this Good News with those who are still perishing and are under the oppression of sins strangle hold. In Jesus' name we pray. Amen

Day 144

> Blessed be the God and Father of our Lord Jesus
> Christ, the Father of mercies and God of all comfort.
> (2 Corinthians 1:3 NKJV)

Because we surround ourselves with the creature comforts this world has to offer we often need continued consolation since they do not fully satisfy. Distress and depression abound in the world around us. Even those who have amassed huge amounts of possessions are disquieted. Even our minds as we attempt to fall asleep at night are turbulent with thoughts the day's activities and those of the days to come. Relief comes through that peace which surpasses all understanding. The mind of him who meditates on Jesus is at peace.

Prayer: Lord God Almighty you are the God of all comfort and the God of all mercy and the Father of our Lord Jesus Christ. Because of you through Christ Jesus we have a blessed hope for our future apart from how dismal the present looks to us and the world around us. Because we live in the world we are tempted to despair as the world does but Father God we are in the world not of the world therefore our trust is in you; not the things of the world. Help us to share this good news with those whom we come in contact that they may share our joy and hope for a bright and blessed future. In Jesus' name we pray. Amen

Day 145

> Likewise, the Spirit helps us in our weakness. For we
> do not know what to pray for as we ought, but the Spirit
> himself intercedes for us with groaning's too deep for
> words. (Romans 8:26 ESV)

God has allowed us to come directly to him in prayer. No longer was a human intercessor needed after the Temple curtain was torn from top to bottom. The Lord gives us dispensation to approach the throne of grace always with all pleas and petitions. We often pray out of selfish motivation rather than praying in God's perfect will. It is then that the Holy Spirit comes to our rescue interceding on our behalf; amending our prayer into one which is God pleasing and in accord with his will.

Prayer: O LORD our Father and our God, there are times when we come to you in prayer not knowing what to pray for or how to pray. Thank you for the intercession of the Holy Spirit who offers up prayer in our behalf. Father you care so intensely for us that even when we cannot pray, you through the third person of your being offer us aid by praying in your will for our every need. What an awesome, loving, caring, gracious and wonderful God you are. Thank you. Hear us O Lord in Jesus' name. Amen

Day 146

> For my thoughts are not your thoughts, neither are
> your ways my ways, declares the Lord. (Isaiah 55:8 NIV)

There are teachings that will tell you they understand the mind of God. How can a carnal minded person understand the mind of God who spoke the world into existence? This is the God who cast the stars into the sky. This is the God who separates night from day and directed the waters of the seas where to stay. This is the God who knits each of us together in the womb. God ways are so far beyond our own that he forgives what we consider unforgivable. God is not definable by man's standards.

Prayer: Father God of creation, your thoughts and ways are far beyond anything we your handmade servants could ever hope to imagine. There are many who seek to be able to trace your thoughts and actions so that they then can say they understand you. No man has the capacity to understand your mind, but we have the capability to attempt to follow your will for our lives and to place our faith in Christ Jesus for our salvation. We can also reach out to one another with love as Christ has directed us to do. Thank you that you are more than man can define because if you were small enough to define then you would not be large enough to worship. Thank you in Jesus' name. Amen

Day 147

> If you obey the commandments of the Lord your God that I command you today, by loving the Lord your God, by walking in his ways, and by keeping his commandments and his statutes and his rules, then you shall live and multiply, and the Lord your God will bless you in the land that you are entering to take possession of it. (Deuteronomy 30:16 ESV)

As we are directed into ever new territory in life we are to observe each of God's commands concerning our daily living. If we walk in the ways of God we will not bring hurt, harm or danger upon one another. God's way always promote concord. God will invoke favor on those who seek to live according to his will.

Prayer: Lord God Almighty, thank you for blessing. Thank you for the blessing of life, love, happiness and the blessed hope of life with you in that prepared place for prepared people. In Jesus' name we pray. Amen

Day 148

> I am the vine; you are the branches. Whoever abides in me and I in him, he it is that bear much fruit, for apart from me you can do nothing. (John 15:5 NIV)

A living union with Christ is essential for the Christian to be effective in life and in ministry. Apart from Christ a person is found to be ineffective. The efforts of those without Christ are as ashes which are blown away by the wind. No thing that is spiritually good can be accomplished in our own strength, but only through Christ Jesus. We can do nothing great or small, think a good thought, speak a good word perform a task whether easy or difficult, we can do nothing apart from Christ.

Prayer: Heavenly Gardener, we are the branches of the vine which is Christ Jesus. Thank you for the nourishing light of your word which enables us to grow. Thank you for pruning away the unproductive portions which sap strength from the vine that could cause fruitlessness. Thank you for the day that is approaching and the fruit which is maturing when the final harvest will take place. Cultivate our lives great gardener God that we may produce a manifold yield. Through Christ Jesus the vine we pray. Amen

Day 149

And which of you by being anxious can add a single hour to his span of life? (Matthew 6:27 NIV)

For many people worry is the order of the day. People worry about traffic in route to a destination. People worry about the outcome of a situation in which they are engaged. People worry over what to eat what not to eat, what to wear what not to wear. Worry is not of God. Worry is of the adversary of this world. It is his deception to make you focus on things which have no control in your life unless you allow them to. Jesus said do not worry about the future for the future has enough worries of its own. Live in the peace of the Lord in the here and now.

Prayer: Eternal, loving and caring God, we children of men tend to let the cares of the world pour in on us like the rush of a flood. Lord we worry about food, shelter, clothing and the wealth of the world. Help your people O God to seek you then they shall know that the worries of this world avail them nothing because you care for them. Lord God you observe our coming and our going, our waking and our slumber.

As we rest in you we need not worry about the next day because you know what lay ahead. In the name of Jesus, we pray. Amen

Day 150

> And I will lead the blind in a way that they do not know,
> in paths that they have not known I will guide them.
> I will turn the darkness before them into light, the
> rough places into level ground. These are the things I
> do, and I do not forsake them. (Isaiah 42:16 ESV)

Our blindness which is caused by the sin which so easily influence's us is causing us to dwell in darkness. We stumble through life as a person with limited sight walking on rocky terrain. Our steps are unsure; we have cause to worry over each step taken because each one could possibly cause severe injury. Thankfully we have a redeeming Savior who will lead his blind unsure people over the rough paths that he will make flat and safe for ambulation. Our Lord will give illumination to those walking in darkness that their feet do not stumble.

Prayer: Lord our light in a darkened land, we are blind and do not know which way to go. Lord like a Good Shepherd you lead us as lost sheep who are blinded by fear. You turn the darkness into light that we might see how to follow you. Where the road is rough you make it level. Thank you, Lord God for being a lamp unto our feet. Thank you, Lord for doing these things for us and not forsaking us unto ourselves. In Jesus' name we pray. Amen

Day 151

> The Lord came and stood there, calling as at the other
> times, "Samuel! Samuel!" Then Samuel said, "Speak, for
> your servant is listening." (1 Samuel 3:10 NIV)

As children of God we must seek to become sensitive to the calling of the Holy Spirit of God as he speaks to us. God speaks to us to share in his work while we are here on this earth. The Lord God speaks to our hearts through the laughter of a child, the embrace of a loved one, the kind words of a stranger and through the warmth of a sunlit day. The Lord speaks to us through his Word as we peruse the scriptures and as we go to him in prayer.

Prayer: O Lord our God, there are many times when you speak to your people yet we do not recognize you. In this life we allow our lives to become focused on family, careers, acquisition of worldly trinkets and self. Forgive us for not acknowledging you as you communicate with us through people, circumstances and your word. Thank you for returning to us over and over and not turning your back on us. Help us to be sensitive to your speaking to us as we walk towards eternity. Through our Lord and savior Jesus Christ we pray this. Amen

Day 152

If you lie down, you will not be afraid; when you lie down, your sleep will be sweet. (Proverbs 3:24 ESV)

The Lord blesses those who are anchored in him with a peace that this world cannot understand. People attempt to sleep at night, yet they are bombarded with intrusive thoughts of the day's activities and the perceived activities of the day to come. To those people who are focused on the Lord and his word there is peace and their minds are at rest as they go to sleep. If you desire restful sleep place your faith in Jesus as Savior, protector and comforter.

Prayer: Lord God of Peace, thank you that through your act of love which came through Christ Jesus we no longer need be afraid and we can lie down in peace and receive sweet peaceful rest. In Jesus name we pray. Amen

Day 153

God said to Moses, "I AM WHO I AM." And he said, "Say this to the people of Israel, 'I am has sent me to you.' " (Exodus 3:14 NIV)

God told Moses his name is I AM WHO I AM. God was saying that he is all that we need in every situation. I AM life and I AM the God you can depend on and trust in says the Lord God Almighty. I AM the one who watches over you as you sleep. I AM the one who opens his hand and provides for you all good things on this earth. I AM the one who will receive you into an eternity of delight which I have prepared for prepared people.

Prayer: Lord God the Great I AM you are powerful and mighty, thank you Lord, for speaking into our lives and saying I AM all you will ever need in this life and into eternity. Through Christ Jesus our Lord and Savior we thank you for being our all and all for all times. Amen

Day 154

Pray then like this: "Our Father in heaven, hallowed be your name. (Matthew 6:9 ESV)

I am not talking about our Father here on earth. I'm not talking about the man that rises each day to go to his labor enabling you to have food and shelter. No, I am not talking about the man that loves us and gives us clothing. No, I am not talking about the man who in our homes seeks to keep us safe checking the doors of the house before he lays down to sleep each night. I am talking about the Father whom the Jews called Jehovah. I'm talking about the Father who the Muslims call Allah. I am talking about the Father whom some address as Yahweh. I am talking about the Father who wrote the Ten Commandment on stone and told Moses to tell the children of Israel my name is "I AM THAT I AM". I am talking about the Father who touched you with the finger of love and allowed you to open your eyes this very morning. I am talking about the Father who will love and care for us, when we don't love and care for ourselves.

Our Father in Heaven, it is wonderful that we have this type of relationship with you. Father God we have earthly fathers who in the pursuit of success deprives us of their presence in our daily lives, but you are always available. We have earthly fathers who abandon their families for grass which seems greener on the other side of the fence, but you O Lord never leave us abandoned. Thank you, Lord God our Abba. In Jesus' name we pray. Amen

Day 155

> He saw that there was no man and wondered that there was no one to intercede; then his own arm brought him salvation, and his righteousness upheld him. (Isaiah 59:16 NIV)

Because of the broken world and mankind's broken fellowship with God, then the inclusion of sin into the world after the fall in the garden caused God displeasure. God knew that salvation could not be implemented into the world through his creation but needed an external source and supply. God took matters into his own hands and came to earth as the man Jesus. Jesus came as a man without sin to bear the sin of the world on an instrument of scorn and shame, offering his life as atonement to the father for forgiveness. Our righteous God worked out a means of righteousness for us that we might be called righteous.

Prayer: Wonderful and Mighty Father God, we thank you that when you looked and saw no one to intercede on behalf of mankind you drew from your being our intercessor, righteous and a savior so that we might receive salvation through you. What an awesome and powerful manifestation of your unmerited grace for sinful men and women. Help us to live with and benefit one another while offering you praise according to the grace which has been bestowed upon us. In Jesus' name we pray. Amen

Day 156

> [19] Therefore go and make disciples of all nations, baptizing them in the name of the Father and of the Son and of the Holy Spirit, [20]and teaching them to obey everything I have commanded you. And surely, I am with you always, to the very end of the age."
> (Matthew 28:19-20 NIV)

The duty of the church is to proclaim the message of salvation to those who have not yet heard the message. The church is not the building where Christians meet each Sunday, but the church is the body of people who meet in that building. Those outside of the body must be challenged to turn their wills and lives over to the risen Christ who died that they too might have a right at eternal life.

Prayer: Lord Jesus it is good that you are forever with us. Thank you for walking beside us in the good times and the bad times. Thank you for being there in sickness and in health and feast and famine. You are such a caring God that you are with us no matter the situation, to strengthen and show your love. Thank you, because of the serenity and security this brings to your people. We pray this Lord Jesus in the name of the Father, Son and Holy Spirit. Amen

Day 157

> I am weary with my moaning; every night I flood my bed with tears; I drench my couch with my weeping.
> (Psalm 6:6 ESV)

We live in a world of trouble. Trouble comes from people who wish to do us harm and trouble comes from poor decisions we make in our own lives. Trouble is on the streets, in our homes, at our jobs, in schools and at church. We are weary from the distress in the world. Comfort seems to never come. If you seek comfort call on the comforter who says "let not your hearts be troubled, I have overcome the world. Seek the peace which Jesus speaks into the lives of those who are his.

Prayer: Father God we live in this veil of tears often not comforting one another and finding no comfort for self. Thank you that Christ Jesus is the comfort for all peoples of this world. When the trying and troubling times arise, Father point us towards Jesus, our comfort and our peace. In Jesus' name we pray. Amen

Day 158

> Though he slay me, I will hope in him; yet I will argue
> my ways to his face. (Job 13:15 ESV)

Whatever God does on our behalf is for our benefit. Every good gift comes from the Lord. We see in the first century many Christians were slain for their belief. Those persons were not slain by the Lord but by the hand of men. If you are faithful to Christ Jesus as your Lord and Savior and he allows you to be slain through an act not of his doing, remember absent from the body present with the Lord.

Prayer: Lord God Almighty, there are so many times when you allow us to be used and abused by the people of this world. Where are you Lord when we are in such terrible pain? Yet surrounded by our struggles we praise you because through you there is vindication. Father thank you for what you are allowing in us. Although we cannot see past our now we know that there is divine orchestration behind those events which shape and mold our character. Lord God help us to understand just like Jesus we too must experience some degree of suffering that we might be tried in the furnace of life. In Jesus' name we pray. Amen

> For no matter how, many promises God has made, they
> are "Yes" in Christ. And so, through him the "Amen" is
> spoken by us to the glory of God. (2 Corinthians 1:20 NIV)

Throughout the Bible we see God giving his divine promises to his creation. God first promised Noah that all life on earth would perish except for all that dwelled on the Ark. God's greatest promise was that he would redeem mankind back to himself. He says he is coming carrying his reward to distribute in accordance with what we have done. God's final promise is "I am coming soon".

Prayer: Thank you, Lord God Almighty that your promises are yes and Amen. By this we have confidence that what you said will not be withheld. You O Lord are a keeper of promise and the promise of life eternal is your greatest promise which we who are in Christ Jesus look forward to. Thank you for being a promise keeper. In Jesus' name we pray. Amen

Day 160

> Consequently, he can save to the uttermost those who draw near to God through him, since he always lives to make intercession for them. (Hebrews 7:25 ESV)

God's precious people will never be without the perfect High Priest Jesus Christ because he lives forever. Christ Jesus intercedes for us before the throne of God, until his return to receive unto himself those who are his. The intervention of Christ weighs in above and beyond any act we can commit on our own.

Prayer: Lord thank you for saving us from the extreme that awaited mankind in eternity. Thank you for the certainty of glory which was prepared for your prepared people. This we pray in the name of the father, Son and Holy Spirit. Amen

Day 161

> And Jesus said to him, "Why do you call me good? No one is good except God alone. (Mark 10:18 ESV)

You have often heard the phrase he is a good man, or she is a good woman. We think of people as being good. People like Mother Theresa, who gave her all to minister to the needy people who were outcasts, we think of similar people as saintly and deserving of a place in the heavenly kingdom. None of our acts of virtue compare with the shed blood of Jesus on Calvary. Goodness comes through Christ alone.

Prayer: Lord God Almighty, we want to think of ourselves as good people because of the things we do in this life. Help us to understand that we dwell in sinful flesh and although we attempt good deeds we still sin in thought, word and deed. Thank you, Lord God for the only human being where there was human goodness found which was in Christ Jesus. In Jesus' name we pray. Amen

Day 162

The Lord is good, a strong hold in the day of trouble; and
he knows them that trust in him. (Nahum 1:7 NKJV)

Trouble does not have an off day. Trouble touches the lives of people daily. Some troubles are minor others are major. During all trouble you face, God is standing there beside you. Trouble is a valley of mayhem where the winds blow and the thunder rumbles but the God we serve quiets the storm and tempers the reverberation of the thunder. Trust the one who commands the world and its elements.

Prayer: O Lord our God in Heaven, you alone are good. You provide us a stronghold in the times of trouble, thank you. You, Father God are aware of those who place their trust in you through Jesus our rock and redeemer. Father our trust in you through our Lord Jesus protects us from being lost and not knowing the way. Through Christ Jesus we pray. Amen

Day 163

Great peace have those who love your law; nothing can
make them stumble. (Psalm 119:165 ESV)

The law teaches us what not to do. If there was no law, we would not
break it. If you are on a road where there is no posted speed limit, then
you can drive as fast or slow as you desire. If you are on a road way
which has a posted speed limit of 75 and you are pulled over for driving
90 then you have broken the law by exceeding the posted limit. God
has set laws for us to live by which gives order to life and enables us to
live in harmony with one another. If you do not break the law, you will
not have a fear of punishment. We break the law through commission
and omission of following God's ordinances. But when you do break
God's law you have a champion in Jesus through whom you can seek
forgiveness which gives the guilty conscience peace.

Prayer: You alone Father God are the God of Shalom, with you through
Christ Jesus Father God we are at peace. But Father our sinful nature
constantly breaks that peace which causes our spirits to grieve our
breach of covenant with you. Father God, thank you for viewing Christ
Jesus in us and continually forgiving us as we walk towards eternity.
In Jesus' name we pray. Amen

Day 164

And he said, "Jesus, remember me when you come into
your kingdom." (Luke 23:42 ESV)

Jesus hung on a cross between two thieves. It was the end of life for all
three as they hung there between earth and heaven. One thief asked
Jesus to remember him, thereby acknowledging his belief in the Son
of God who came to offer salvation to a sin darkened world. If there
is opportunity to seek forgiveness and proclaim Jesus as your savior,
you can be saved. But why wait until the 11th hour? No one knows the

day, or the hour of their demise so seek Christ while the blood runs warm in your veins.

Prayer: Lord Jesus, we are guilty, and we confess our sinfulness. Our prayer is for your forgiveness because you were required to shed your blood for us. Lord remember us when you return to carry those who are called by your name back to your kingdom. You, Lord Jesus are our Lord and our God. For your name's sake we pray. Amen

Day 165

> When Jesus therefore had received the vinegar, he said, It is finished: and he bowed his head, and gave up the ghost. (John 19:30 KJV)

Jesus accepted the death due mankind for the sin mankind committed. We should be ever thankful that we do not get what we deserve for our sinful activities. We do not have to pay the price. Jesus paid the price for us. By dying Jesus carried our sins to the grave. By rising Jesus offers us the opportunity to one day also rise for a new life with him in eternity.

Prayer: Thank you Lord God Almighty for the life, death and resurrection of Christ Jesus. In Jesus' name we pray. Amen

Day 166

> If we confess our sins, he is faithful and just to forgive us our sins and to cleanse us from all unrighteousness. (1 John 1:9 KJV)

Sin is everywhere; we cannot escape it. As we go about our daily business sin is crouching like a tiger ready to spring from the recesses of darkness to subdue, entangle and consume you. As you first become conscious of sin's manifestation in your life cast the light of conscious confession upon it which dilutes its hold and power over you. Ask the

Lord that you not repeat that sin again, saying "Lord deliver me from evil".

Prayer: Father God in Heaven, we come confessing our sin right now. Lord, investigate our hearts and remove the sins which we are unaware of and cannot confess; cast them into oblivion that we may never again embrace those things which remove us from relationship with you. Father God help us to turn our backs on the sins of commission and the sins of omission which temps us. Hear us Lord for the sake of Christ Jesus who died for our sins. In Jesus' name we pray. Amen

Day 167

> John answered and said, "A man can receive nothing unless it has been given to him from heaven. (John 3:27 NKJV)

Envy is in direct conflict with the 9th and 10th Commandments of God. When we envy, we want what the other person has. In wanting what others have, we are, saying to God "What you have given me is deficient". Whatever happens in life is a result of God's benevolence. What God gives he gives. What God withholds he withholds. God provides as he deems appropriate.

Prayer: Lord God of provision, we children of men reach out to grasp the things of the world yet everything we have is ordained by heaven. Help us to understand where our possessions, achievements, life and even love come from. Thank you, Lord for constantly giving even while we gather and do not share with our fellowman or give you a proper offering in return. Lord thank you for the ultimate provision of life through Christ Jesus. In his name we pray. Amen

Day 168

> But for you who revere my name, the sun of righteousness will rise with healing in its wings. And

you will go out and leap like calves released from the
stall. (Malachi 4:2 NIV)

The day is coming when all mankind will see the earth being scorched.
Those who are at that time still walking in darkness willfully sinning
will be consumed. For those who have faith in Jesus and who are in
right relationship with him that day will be like walking to sunshine
after standing in a frigid place. Those in Christ will feel the warmth of
his love as those who reject him will sear. God's people will be restored
to a pristine eternity awaiting them.

Prayer: Awesome and Mighty God our creator, your name is to be
worshipped. Your acts of grace, mercy and love are inspiring. Father
we eagerly wait for your healing of the illness of the land as we still
walk in the darkness of sin. Father we await the sun of righteousness
with its healing that will come with the Son upon his return. Thank
you, Father God that one day we will leap for joy at the arrival of our
Lord Jesus as he comes to claim us for our eternal home with you in
that prepared place for your prepared people. In Jesus' name we pray.
Amen

Day 169

Beloved, let us love one another: for love is of God; and
everyone who loves is born of God, and knows God.
(1 John 4:7 NRSV)

Love is a loosely used word in our society. People profess love to get
other people to indulge their desires. True love requires nothing in
return. True love has no hidden agenda. True love is generated by the
Holy Spirit of God which dwells in the heart. True love is evidence that
you are walking with God because God is love.

Prayer: God of love, we children of men tend to sparingly give our
love to one another. Often our offering of love is predicated upon an
exchange. For many of us our gift of love requires the other person to

give some tangible item or act for the exchange to take effect. Mankind loves because of, but you O Lord Loves "In Spite Of". Thank you, Lord God that you love "In Spite Of". Help us to stop loving because of. Help us to offer love as you do, without reciprocal payment. Through Christ Jesus the ultimate act of love you offered us we pray this prayer. Amen

Day 170

> By faith Noah, being warned by God concerning events
> as yet unseen, in reverent fear constructed an ark for
> the saving of his household. By this he condemned the
> world and became an heir of the righteousness that
> comes by faith. (Hebrews 11:7 ESV)

It was an act of faith that prompted Noah to build a vessel in a landlocked area where it was known no huge amount of water would accumulate. Noah believed God's word. God has given us his word through the sixty-six books of the Bible. When you believe what is written in the Bible it is an act of faith. Faith believes in what cannot be experienced through the human senses. When Christ comes faith will vindicate the believer; the lack of faith will cause the unbeliever to be judged.

Prayer: Holy Father God we children of men have been given warning that Christ will return and upon his return the world as we know it will be consumed by fire. Lord God as the warning was given to Noah before the world was consumed by the flood; he heeded, by building an ark to save those whom you ordained as salvageable. Help all mankind to build their ark on faith in Christ Jesus. Let your Holy Spirit revive people everywhere to heed the warning and believe in Jesus and be saved. In Jesus' name we pray. Amen

Day 171

> Do not lay up for yourselves treasures on earth, where
> moth and rust destroy and where thieves break in and
> steal. (Matthew 6:19 NKJV)

Life has taught people that he who acquires the most marbles is the winner in this life. There are people who learned through natural disaster, theft or other catastrophe that stuff is just that, "stuff". There is nothing on this earth we will carry into the grave with us. There is neither a Moving Van nor Armored Car following the hearse to the cemetery. Loosely embrace the wealth and trinkets of this world. Our true treasure is stored in Heaven awaiting us.

Prayer: Father God, we accumulate many things in life while we inhabit this earth. If the question is asked "where do, you live" we give an address with city, state and street. This is the place where we keep our earthly accumulations. Lord help us to not place such a high value on the things we have and become so attached to that our focus of you become clouded. Help us Lord God to treasure that which is not now seen but will one day come with the arrival of Christ our Savior. In Jesus' name we pray. Amen

Day 172

> If you know that he is righteous, you may be sure that
> everyone who practices righteousness has been born
> of him. (1 John 2:29 ESV)

As a member of God's family, you are marked by his Holy nature. This nature permeates your language, thoughts, actions and people who encounter you can detect it on you, although they may not understand it. God's Holy nature exudes righteousness. Any righteousness we possess is not of our own making but that of Christ Jesus who because of his sacrifice for us now makes us righteous. Our standards of behaviors are governed by our Lord Jesus who demonstrates appropriate actions.

Prayer: Lord God Almighty, we look to Christ Jesus who is the righteousness of the earth for guidance. Help us by the power of your Holy Spirit to be reborn of Christ Jesus so we may practice righteousness. Lord we desire to be born of the righteousness found only in Christ Jesus who leads us in the paths of righteousness. In Jesus' name we pray. Amen

Day 173

give thanks in all circumstances; for this is the will of
God in Christ Jesus for you. (1Thessalonians 5:18 ESV)

A thankful heart is the mark of a joyful Christian. God has done, is doing and will do much in our lives. No matter the circumstance the Christian has an unshakeable joy which the world does not understand. This joy comes from reflecting on the God who created all things. So, when the worlds throw's trials your way, don't tell God about your trials. Tell your trials about your God.

Prayer: Our Father in Heaven, as we progress through this life there may be many clouds which rain on our parades. There may be times of great distress, turmoil and uncertainty. There may be lost opportunities, lost relationships and lost love. Lord there may be times when the desire to embrace temptation is almost stronger than the desire to live according to your word. Thank you, Lord, in the name of Jesus that when going through those tough times we can thank you for the reassurance that you are there every step of the way. Looking back Lord we know that if it had not been for you we would have faltered and fell. Lord thank you for the strength which enables us not to complain. We offer thanks in Jesus' name. Amen

Day 174

The Lord will fulfill his purpose for me; your steadfast
love, O Lord, endures forever. Do not forsake the work
of your hands. (Psalm 138:8 ESV)

You are the work of God's hand his personal creation made in his image. God will not abandon you. Even among trouble which may befall the child of God they are protected by an unseen force of divine protective security. God has a purpose for each life that he allows on this earth. His love for his children and his purpose for his created children is that they may receive everlasting life to live with him into eternity.

Prayer: Almighty loving and Merciful God, our lives are but a flicker in the scheme of time. Lord God while we have life and breath let our purpose be that of giving focus and direction to those who do not have a relationship with you through Christ Jesus. Enable us O God to reach out in love to those still wandering souls who are caught up in this world, so that they may be privileged to your divine protection and one day live with you in glory forever. In Jesus' name we pray. Amen

Day 175

> Keep your life free from love of money, and be content
> with what you have, for he has said, "I will never leave
> you nor forsake you." (Hebrews 13:5 ESV)

This world teaches that you must do whatever is necessary to get money and we see what money can buy, leading us to want it. We all need money to live on. And we should strive to live within our means. Today there are many who ought to say, "I wish the jones' quit buying things I can't afford". What God gives you is enough for you. God is always there.

Prayer: Heavenly Father Our Lord and our God, we offer thanks for your never-ending presence in our lives. Lord how could we ever offer enough thanks for what you have done, is doing and will do in our lives. In Jesus' name we pray. Amen

Day 176

No, in all these things we are more than conquerors
through him who loved us. (Romans 8:37 NIV)

When hardships befall you how do you respond? There is the story of
the three Hebrew boys being cast into the fiery furnace. It was their
faith in an awesome God which protected them in their hardship. Be
not like the person who would say "God why are you letting this happen
to me"? Be like the person who would say "Lord, I don't understand
how but I know through this you will be glorified because I trust you".
Do not take ownership of the hardship but overcome it with faith in
God's wonder working power. Then claim the victory which awaits
you. In many cases hardships are opportunities to exercise your faith.
Properly, placed faith produces positive results.

Prayer: Gracious God our Father, we have the daunting task of being
on constant guard against the enemy who brings trial and tribulation
into this world. Father God we get knocked down, but we can arise
again in Christ Jesus. O God for those who do not know Jesus, when the
waves of opposition accost them they sink into the situation as if in a
bog. Thank you for Christ the solid rock upon which we find support
in the mire of the quicksand of adversity. Let those who do not know
Christ as a restorer be touched in a way which leaves no doubt in their
minds that he is the epitome of love and restoration for all mankind.
In Jesus' name we pray. Amen

Day 177

But I do not account my life of any value nor as precious
to myself, if only I may finish my course and the
ministry that I received from the Lord Jesus, to testify
to the gospel of the grace of God. (Acts 20:24 ESV)

We are in a race which spans the sequences of our lives. This is a
marathon not a sprint. During the daily grind of this race we will

encounter slips, falls, nudges and obstacles which will impede and delay us. We must press on despite the hardship. We must endure until the final lap of this lifelong race is run. In the end as a testimony to the goodness of God, our lives will then reflect his enduring love in our lives. Jesus will come and give us rest.

Prayer: Lord, we encounter daily problems in our lives. Teach our hearts to turn to Jesus as the model which will give us guidance and strength in the trying and troubling times. Lord, let your people know in their inner being that Jesus is all they need to overcome the challenges of life. In Jesus name we pray. Amen

Day 178

For we walk by faith, not by sight. (2 Corinthians 5:7 NKJV)

We live in a world where seeing is believing. However due to technological advances in optics and audio broadcasting things can be manipulated to display almost any imaginable concept. Moving in faith does not require seeing with mortal eyes. Moving in faith requires us to travel with spiritual eyes. Faith says, "I don't see it in the natural, but I know it is there in the spiritual". With faith you see it before you see it.

Prayer: Lord God our Father, our faith looks trustingly to the lamb of Calvary. Father God we cannot do life alone under our own power and in our own authority. You knew this, and you have instilled in the hearts of those who are yours that they must rely on a power greater than themselves. For us Lord God that power is found in Christ Jesus alone. Bless us with unyielding faith. Amplify our faith that we may share its results with a still lost world. In Jesus' name we pray. Amen

Day 179

You therefore must be perfect, as your heavenly Father is perfect. (Matthew 5:48 ESV)

We have an example for which we can aspire, that is to be perfect. This perfection is not gauged by earthly standards but by the heavenly standards established through God. This heavenly standard of perfection is unattainable for mortals. Anything less than perfection is not pleasing to our Holy Father God because God is perfection. Mankind cannot gain perfection through its own volition; God cannot accept anything less than perfection. If God accepted less, then perfection then he would be imperfect which is not in his character. Therefore, we keep struggling with our imperfections trying each day to be a little better than the day before. Our perfection is found in Christ Jesus.

Prayer: Heavenly Father God, we your children strive for perfection in our day to day vocations. We strive to be the best employee, father, mother, mentor or whatever endeavor we pursue. Guide us in the pursuit of heavenly perfection while we are still on the earth. Father God, if we could just obtain a small portion of the heavenly perfection, this world as we know it would be a wonderful place for every man, woman, boy and girl. Father God hear our prayer in Jesus' name. Amen

Day 181

[11]Do not speak evil against one another, brothers and sisters. Whoever speaks evil against another or judges another, speaks evil against the law and judges the law; but if you judge the law, you are not a doer of the law but a judge. [12]There is one lawgiver and judge who is able to save and to destroy. So, who, then, are you to judge your neighbor? (James 4:11-12 NRSV)

"You are no good, worthless, and good for nothing". If you have not spoken these words certainly you have heard others speak them of another of God's children. How quick we are to cast judgment on one another. Regardless of ethnicity, political views, religious inclinations or gender, if we would take the time to carefully, scrutinize our own actions we certainly would not have time to criticize one another.

God made all people in his image and the image of God declares all as his precious children. This includes Black men, White men, Asian, Indian, Latino and all in between. We should diligently seek to clean up our own act and judge self only. When we attempt to judge others, we defile the law of love as Jesus gave it in **Matt. 22:37-40.** How can you afford to judge another when you cannot control self? Love one another as Christ loved us; do not judge one another.

Prayer: Lord God Our Redeemer, thank you for another day and the ability to interact with our brothers and sisters in this world. We thank you for the love displayed by your children. Help all to love one another as you love. In Jesus' name we pray. Amen

Day 182

> I was ready to be sought by those who did not ask for me; I was ready to be found by those who did not seek me. I said, "Here am I, here am I," to a nation that was not called by my name. (Isaiah 65:1 ESV)

Like Israel we outwardly seek God but, on the inside, we secretly desire to continue with clandestine acts of the flesh hoping to never get caught by someone who would call us to accountability. If we were judged by another human being, we would stand wholeheartedly guilty without the benefit of mercy. But we are not judged by men we are judged by an infinite and eternal God who seeks to cleanse us and one day carry us home to be with him.

Prayer: God of compassion and love, how can we ever thank you enough for seeking us out as the "Good Shepherd"? Father you sought us as the Christ seeking that which was lost. You sought us out individually and collectively until you found us wandering in the darkness of our sinful lives, then you gently carried us back to the safety of the flock. Father we offer to you our lives as a testimony of the gratitude we have for your unending quest of love for your flock. In Jesus' name we pray. Amen

Day 183

But even if we or an angel from heaven should preach
to you a gospel contrary to the one we preached to you,
let him be accursed. (Galatians 1:8 ESV)

People want to hear what they want to hear. When the conversation turns to something less than what is pleasing to the ear people tend to reject that conversation for one which pleases them. The Gospel of Jesus Christ is not up to adaptation to fit human desire. The Gospel of Jesus Christ is God's inerrant Word which is established as a guide by which all mankind can gauge his actions in this life. The Gospel tells us what God has done for us, is doing for us and will do for us. Through the hearing of the Gospel we then can emulate it and live with and for one another to demonstrate our love for the Triune God.

Prayer: Father God in Heaven, it is by the power of the Good News that we children of men have knowledge of the salvation found in Christ Jesus. Lord God that Good News changes lives and brings sinners to repentance. Father let the truth of your Word continually touch our hearts and draw all people to Christ the Salvation of the world. In Jesus' name we pray. Amen

Day 184

Wake up from your drunken stupor, as is right, and do
not go on sinning. For some have no knowledge of God.
I say this to your shame. (1 Corinthians 15:34 ESV)

If you have ever drank too much alcohol, then you know what it is to act out in misguided judgement. Alcohol has a way of changing a person and making them act in ways which are not necessarily acceptable. The world identifies them as being drunk. Many are drunk on the ways of the world which far exceed alcohol. The world seduces people into actions contrary to God's will for mankind which is not acceptable to

God but approved by the world. We are called to become clear-headed again following God's law and not the worlds enticements.

Prayer: Dear God our Father and Creator, many are the times we forget to look to you for guidance. It is at those times of failing to see you that we fall into sinful acts which burden our souls, cause our expression to sadden and separate us from you and other of your children. Lord God Almighty do not let us be like those who do not know you but let us in everything seek you first for direction so that we will not be put to shame. Father in the name of Jesus we ask this. Amen

Day 185

> Beloved, let us love one another, for love is from God,
> and whoever loves has been born of God and knows
> God. (1 John 4:7 ESV)

There are people who don't look like you, think like you, talk like you believe what you believe or live in the neighborhood you live in. We must remember all things were created through Jesus which includes "those other people". We cannot harden our hearts against people who are different because we disagree with their agenda. Our creator God is awaiting your receptiveness to the new malleable heart he desires to give you. The LORD God will only give it to those who desire to live according to his command "Love your neighbor as yourself". Jesus says, "Love one another as I have loved you". If you allow him, he will replace your hardened heart with a new workable heart of compassion.

Prayer: Merciful God of Love, work in the hearts of your people the ability to love one another as you have loved us. Father God we cannot truthfully say we know you if we do not love one another. Birth in us the spirit of unconditional love Lord God. In Jesus' name we ask this. Amen

Day 186

For godly grief produces a repentance that leads
to salvation without regret, whereas worldly grief
produces death. (2 Corinthians 7:10 ESV)

You must believe that God through Christ Jesus has forgiven you your sin. This belief is not of your own doing it comes from a relationship with God the Father nurtured and cultivated by the Holy Spirit. Faith works forgiveness in the heart of the repentant person. Faith in Christ, not in regret for wrong action is the only confidence we have for forgiveness.

Prayer: O Merciful God our Father in Heaven, in our daily walk we experience conflict with other people with whom we come in contact. Many times, after such conflict we feel sorrowful for our actions, words and thoughts. Father just as we can repent to our fellowman help us to sincerely repent to you for our misdeeds, harsh words and sinful thoughts. Father God lead us to the cross of Calvary so there we might confess our sin to the one who died in our place as we are being led towards salvation in his name. Through Christ Jesus we pray. Amen

Day 187

I want to know Christ and the power of his resurrection
and the fellowship of sharing in his sufferings,
becoming like him in his death. (Philippians 3:10 NIV)

When we say we want to know Christ we are saying we desire a change in who we are. In knowing Christ, we change into new creations, living a different way which promotes, kindness, grace, mercy and love. Everything about a person changes when they come to know Christ Jesus as Lord and Savior. The power of Jesus' resurrection is hope in the life everlasting that he has awaiting those who are his. As the Spirit of God who raised Christ from the dead comes to reside with you, it raises you from the spiritually dead life of sin and will raise you from a physical death at the resurrection when Jesus returns to collect his people for eternity.

Prayer: Our Father in Heaven, on this earth there are many who hold administrative authority in the palm of their hands. For these men and women, they wield within their sphere of influence their power like demigods; requiring those under their purview to yield to their supremacy. Lord God Almighty, direct all people to know Christ Jesus and the power of his resurrection. Let us in unison Father God, be in fellowship with his suffering that one day we may become like him in his death. Lord in your mercy, hear our prayer. This we ask in Jesus' name. Amen

Day 188

> For I decided to know nothing among you except Jesus
> Christ and him crucified. (1 Corinthians 2:2 ESV)

In this world of information overload, it is difficult to remain focused on one thing for any length of time. The human mind in inundated with intrusive thoughts which arise without any formal warning. Even in prayer sometimes we must with great effort stay on course as we speak to the Lord. Seek a quiet place where you can focus on meditating on the goodness of Christ Jesus and his resurrection. If you make a conscious decision to focus on Christ a great power will come to your aid.

Prayer: Heavenly Father, thank you for coming in the flesh because of the love you have for your hand made servants. Thank you that salvation is offered through the sacrificial suffering and death of Jesus Christ for the forgiveness of sins. We rejoice because of your unmerited love for us. In Jesus' name we pray. Amen

Day 189

Judge not, and you will not be judged; condemn not,
and you will not be condemned; forgive, and you will
be forgiven. (Luke 6:37 ESV)

It is easy to view, point out and reflect on the shortcomings of our fellow men and women. We are to love the unlovable person. The reason we cannot love a person is because of our biased opinion of that person which is, judgmental. We can illuminate the darkness of sin by being that light which guides others to seek the path to righteousness. If we are to judge someone we cannot use mankind as a gauge but let Christ alone be the gauge by which we judge ourselves and not any other.

Prayer: Almighty Father and everlasting God, forgive us for being so judgmental towards one another. We can easily condemn another for their infractions of societal standards yet when we are caught in that same scenario we demand mercy when society demands justice. Help us to forgive one another as you have forgiven us through Christ Jesus. In Jesus' name we pray. Amen

Day 190

Blessed be the God and Father of our Lord Jesus
Christ, the Father of mercies and God of all comfort.
(2 Corinthians 1:3 NKJV)

When distress plagues our lives, we have two choices as a resolution to dealing with the affliction which confronts us. We can run to another human being who we think can solve our dilemma or we can take our problem to the one who created the heavens and the earth. Christ our comfort gives us consolation, relief and encouragement during times of difficulty. No man or woman can offer the calm afforded by the Lord of Lords and King of Kings.

Prayer: God of all comfort we thank you for being there in the times of trouble. Thank you for giving us the spirit of recognition which enables us to place our trust in you even when we cannot see or know the way to go. Thank you that you have worked in our lives in such a way that we intimately know you and live through your divine guidance. Lord you make the dark places light and the crooked places straight. Thank you for your grace which protects calms and provides for us. In Jesus' name we pray. Amen

Day 191

> The Lord is good, a stronghold in the day of trouble; he
> knows those who take refuge in him. (Nahum 1:7 ESV)

Trouble is a portion of life that is unavoidable. From the womb to the tomb we each experience our share of life's troubles and then we die. Operating under the might of our strength, we are constantly knocked off our center, finding it difficult to recover when life bombards us with difficulty. The only way to step up to the challenge is to allow God to control the outcome and faithfully rely on him for and end result which will benefit you now or in the future.

Prayer: Lord God Almighty, you are good to us as we experience trouble in this life. Our troubles are shared by you as we call on the name of Jesus. Help us to help our brothers and sisters who do not know Christ, him who was crucified, to call on him also. Father give us the ability to speak the words which will ignite a burning desire in others to know Jesus the one who died for all mankind. In Jesus' name we pray. Amen

Day 192

> For many are called, but few are chosen.
> (Matthew 22:14 NKJV)

How many times have you felt in inner urge to tell someone about the love of God, only to shrink back out of fear of rejection, fear of ridicule or shame because of the company you were in? Each person who has been buried in the waters of baptism, have the indwelling Holy Spirit of God which calls us to deliver the message of Christ crucified. Do you respond to the inner call of God? Some even think they are receiving the call, in error because they are so sinful that God cannot possibly be calling them to task. The truth is all have sinned and fall short of the Glory of God. God chooses whom he will for the building of his kingdom. God's invitation marks you as his chosen.

Prayer: Father God you have issued the invitation to come to the wedding feast of the Lamb, but many are too busy with the cares of this world. Many think the invitation has been sent in error because they have blemishes on their lives, which they believe cannot be forgiven. Many are just rebellious and do not accept your invitation. Give the spirit of discernment to the arrogant, spiritually ill, addicted, poor, abusive and those who think themselves self-sufficient, so they too will come to the feast. Thank you, Lord for accepting us just as we are, your sinful and unclean created servants. In Jesus' name we pray. Amen

Day 193

> And the King will answer them, 'Truly, I say to you, as
> you did it to one of the least of these my brothers, you
> did it to me.' (Matthew 25:40 ESV)

God has blessed each of us with a gift. This gift is a resource which we can use to better the lives of other people around us. You may think to yourself, I have so little supply for self that I cannot offer what I have, or I will be found wanting. The truth is God will supply all your needs when you seek to aid those who have less than you. Through his grace you will find that your needs will be met. We reap what we sow; give and it will be given back compounded.

Prayer: Father God you have given us the power to aid and defend the powerless. There are those who are less fortunate than ourselves and we must never turn a blind eye to the needs of those who have fell on hard times. Lord you have called every Christian to the duty of aid for another of your children. Lord God as Christ aided those in need help us to do likewise. Lord you provide for and defend the powerless and call us to follow that example. Help us Lord God Almighty to step up and answer the call. In Jesus' name we pray this. Amen

Day 194

> Only hold on to what you have until I come.
> (Revelation 2:25 NIV)

We get so easily caught up in the activities of this world that we forget we will one day be held accountable to the creator of our existence. We see other people doing those things which are pleasing to the senses which give them satisfaction and pleasure. After reflecting on past activities, we sometimes regret having participated in that activity because we now know it was out of the lust of the flesh which sought pleasure, success, revenge, or materialism that we engaged in those activities. Because of our actions we may have inflicted upon someone damage, pain, injury, affliction or even death.

Prayer: Father God, this is not our home we are but travelers passing through this barren land. As your children we anxiously await the time when we will be taken home to live in that place Jesus has prepared for us. Our Lord Jesus promised that our pain, sorrow suffering and tears due to our sinful nature would one day be banished. An unspeakable joy awaits us upon his return. Until then we wait, we hope, and we pray for better days which lie ahead. In Jesus' name we pray. Amen

Day 195

> Behold, upon the mountains, the feet of him who brings good news, who publishes peace! Keep your feasts, O Judah; fulfill your vows, for never again shall the worthless pass through you; he is utterly cut off.
> (Nahum 1:15 ESV)

The one who brings the Good News of the Gospel brings peace to the troubled conscious of the people of earth. It is the message of Christ and him crucified which gives that peace which surpasses all understanding. An even greater message is that of his resurrection which encourages us to know that as we look to him for salvation we too will one day be resurrected.

Prayer: Father God almighty, it is always good for us when we receive good news. Thank you for the Good news which is shared with us each and every Sunday morning in worship service. Thank you for the Good News which is given us through your Word. Empower us to be the bearers of Good News to those who are struggling with life on life's terms. Help us to deliver the Good News of Christ's deliverance through your Grace. This we ask in Jesus' name. Amen

Day 196

You keep him in perfect peace whose mind is stayed on you, because he trusts in you. (Isaiah 26:3 ESV)

Peace is highly sought after, inward peace, outward peace, peace in the home, on the job at school, in the church and peace with God. Peace for mankind comes through Jesus Christ for those who are willing to accept it. Jesus, the "Prince of Peace" brings calmness to troubled lives in this hectic world. Keep your mind on Jesus, he can call the raging water and wind back to peace so can he call your troubled mind to receive peace.

Prayer: Lord God our Protector and our Comfort, all too often people look to themselves to resolve the many problems this life presents them with. It is only after things go haywire that people then realize that their trust has been misplaced. Thank you for keeping us in perfect peace when we allow our minds to reflect on you and allow you to solve the problems of life. Father enable us to frustrate the adversary by removing the weapons of doubt and agitation that he attempts to plant in our hearts and minds. Lord God Almighty we thank you this day for the ultimate peace of Christ our Salvation. This we pray in the name of the Father, Son and Holy Spirit. Amen

Day 197

The Lord God took the man and put him in the Garden
of Eden to work it and keep it. (Genesis 2:15 ESV)

In the beginning God gave mankind an assignment to care for the earth as he first placed Adam in the Garden of Eden to care for it. Our mission is to give attention to all vegetation that is on the earth. We are to use it for our benefit as healing herbs, food for the body fragrances for our sense of smell and coverings from the heat of the day. As we finish our assigned duties and relax surrounded by God's natural foliage, we are operating in his will to work and keep this world as he has told us to do.

Prayer: Lord God our Provider, you have given us this earth to subdue it and to rule over every living creature. We, Father God are your stewards over your creation. Thank you for giving us such an important responsibility. You alone O God gave us the ability to develop gardening, tools, cities, textiles, technology and music. Forgive us for corrupting what was supposed to be done for the good of all and to your glory. With the good came bad as we used the good for evil such as murder, theft, vengeance and death. Help us Father God to return to offering care for this earth and each other which you first commissioned us to carry out. And Father may we do everything which rises as a fragrant offering to you. In Jesus' name we pray. Amen

Day 198

I call heaven and earth to witness against you today,
that I have set before you life and death, blessing
and curse. Therefore, choose life, that you and your
offspring may live. (Deuteronomy 30:19 ESV)

God has given us a choice of direction for our lives. God will not force on us what is better, but he gives us the opportunity of free will choice. We can choose to follow the ways of the world that many say is acceptable, and you must be true to yourself. Being true to you does not mean harming yourself spiritually and physically. Through Christ Jesus God has given us the opportunity for life now and into eternity. Jesus said he has come to give us an abundant life, choose it.

Prayer: God of life, we children of men often feed the little sins in our life which we indulge and allow growing into unmanageable sin which then consume us. Help us to starve the little sins and nurture the wholesome attitudes taught us by Christ. Help us O God in our daily walk. In Jesus' name we pray. Amen

Day 199

> And he said: "Naked I came from my mother's womb, And naked shall I return there. The LORD gave, and the LORD has taken away; Blessed be the name of the LORD." (Job 1:21 NKJV)

Everything we have is the direct result of God's divine intervention. People will say "I earned this through the sweat of my brow and hard work". They forget that it is God who gives us the ability to accumulate wealth. We came into this world with nothing and we will leave this world in the same manner.

Prayer: Heavenly Father, trouble in this life is one thing which we your created servants cannot escape. We look upon the works of our hands as they disintegrate before our eyes and we gasp in unbelief that this could happen to us. Lord it is only through our relationship with you that we can stand under the pressures associated with the turmoil of this life. Let those who see us who are stable enough to stand fast in times of trouble seek to stand on that same solid rock where you are found. Help us to share the Good News of Christ the solid Rock upon which we stand; all other ground is sinking sand. Through Christ Jesus our solid Rock we pray. Amen

Day 200

Humble yourselves, therefore, under the mighty hand
of God so that at the proper time he may exalt you.
(1 Peter 5:6 ESV)

In society today, we are pitted against one another in every aspect of life. In school our children are in competition to see who can gain acknowledgment on the "Honor Role". In the classroom the one with the highest grades receive the acclaim from the teacher. In the workplace the one who presents the work assigned to him in a manner which illustrates competence beyond the requirements of the company receive awards. In the church the person who knows the most Bible verses is looked upon as the Bible scholar. In each of these instances people become puffed up and prideful. Let us ask God to keep us humble.

Prayer: Lord God Almighty, Creator of Heaven and Earth, you allow your people the opportunity of earthly success but in some cases, we become overly puffed up and conceited in our achievements. Father God give us a humble Spirit that we not become prideful; undervaluing others. Lord in your mercy and in Jesus' name hear our prayer. Amen

Day 201

It is better to take refuge in the Lord than to trust in
man. (Psalm 118:8 NIV)

It seems that sometimes people take pleasure inflicting pain upon one another. You see this from a very young age as children act out cruelly towards one another. This carries over into adulthood as people devise mischievous acts as a ruse which brings embarrassment and sometime harm to the targeted individual. At other times people spread slanderous gossip, outright lies and derogatory information to discredit another human being. Although we are sinful creatures made in the image of God he would never mistreat us as we mistreat one another. God creates concord not discord. Let us seek to be like minded.

Prayer: Lord of Harmony, it is always frustrating when we are harmed by people whom we think we can trust. Lord your word says to love your enemy. In life those who harm us are not always viewed as our enemy. Help us to love those we perceive as unlovable. Give us the power to overcome the pain and hurt. Enable us to extend the hand of friendship and the embrace of love. In Jesus' name, our peace we ask this. Amen

Day 202

> And he arose and came to his father. But while he was still a long way off, his father saw him and felt compassion, and ran and embraced him and kissed him. (Luke 15:20 ESV)

Like the Prodigal Son we want to do things our way. We go off in the direction our lustful flesh takes us and then when we find that our actions have brought us to a place of devastation we look around and ask the question, "what went wrong"? Fortunately, some come to the realization that they in their own power lack focus, discipline or the knowledge to correct their now materially, physically or mentally impoverished situation. It is at those times when "God our loving Father" comes to us to carry us to the comfort and security of being home with him. We must look to "Our Father in Heaven" from whom all blessings flow.

Prayer: Father God, we move through life often making mistakes which take us out of alignment with your word. We then seek to be restored by trying to find you although engulfed in our misdeeds. Like a ship lost in the fog without it's navigation devices we wander aimlessly until you come to us and comfort us in our dilemma. Thank you, Lord, our God for seeking us out. In Jesus' name we offer our praise and gratitude. Amen

Day 203

> I know, my God, that you test the heart and have
> pleasure in uprightness. In the uprightness of my heart
> I have freely offered all these things, and now I have
> seen your people, who are present here, offering freely
> and joyously to you. (1 Chronicles 29:17 ESV)

God is pleased with integrity and generosity in his people. When you walk in honesty, God smiles on you and the works of your hands. As he enables you through good works to gain wealth you must remember that God blesses us that we can bless others. Therefore, we are to give back to God what he has given us. We can give by sharing with the less fortunate or giving to God's work in the kingdom.

Prayer: O Lord God, you test the hearts of your children. Father you are pleased in uprightness and the rejection of deceit. Give us O God a heart pleasing to you. Help us to come before you freely and offer our hearts as a monument to the work you are accomplishing in and through us. In the name of Jesus, we pray. Amen

Day 204

> Bear with each other and forgive whatever grievances
> you may have against one another. Forgive as the Lord
> forgave you. (Colossians 3:13 NIV)

It is not always easy to forgive someone who has hurt you. People live for years with resentment in their hearts for past wrongs committed against them by another. If we are brutally honest with ourselves, we too are the culprit of harming others through our actions and words. As we want to be forgiven we ought to forgive others. At the very least we ask God for forgiveness shouldn't we forgive others in the same manner as God forgives, which is unconditionally if we ask it of him.

Prayer: Lord God our Father in Heaven, your word encourages us to forgive those who have grieved us. O God in our weakness we cannot do this under our own authority we cannot wipe the slate clean, there is always a smudge left which reminds us again. But Father if the truth is told without your continued forgiveness we all would be lost. Strengthen us O God in our frailty. Help us O Lord to bear with each other. Help us O forgiver of the world to forgive each other. Help us to forgive as you have forgiven us. In Jesus' name, we pray. Amen

Day 205

> Be very careful, then, how you live--not as unwise but as wise, [16] making the most of every opportunity, because the days are evil. (Ephesians 5:15-16 NIV)

As children of God also called children of light we are to be careful how we live out our lives on this earth. We are to shun what we know to be the ways of darkness and seek to know only the ways of light which are ordained by the Lord. If we seek the Lord in all thing's, then we will be given the option of light rather than darkness. Light is the way of wisdom. Darkness is the way of foolishness which leads to destruction. We must take care how we live because if we profess Christianity and live as the world lives then we are not presenting a good example in our walk.

Prayer: Lord God Almighty we live in a world tainted with the hue of evil. There is darkness all around. Guide your People O God to display wisdom of speech, thought and action. Allow the light of your goodness to radiate from those who are called by your name as they travel through the darkness. Permit your people to be that beacon in the darkened recesses of this earth, shedding light to guide all who seek Christ as savior. Lord in your mercy Hear our prayer. In Jesus' name, we pray. Amen

Day 206

> But when Jesus saw it, He was greatly displeased and
> said to them, "Let the little children come to Me, and
> do not forbid them; for of such is the kingdom of God.
> (Mark 10:14 NKJV)

Jesus was adamant about praying for and blessing the children in his vicinity. Children are a blessing from God, created from the love of two individuals to become one new person in the kingdom. Jesus laid Holy Hands on the children and stated for such is the kingdom of Heaven. Jesus wasn't saying that Heaven is inhabited by children. Jesus was saying with the innocence and acceptance possessed by a child, so is the innocence and confidence in Christ Jesus of those who will inhabit Heaven.

Prayer: Heavenly Father God, all your children are created in your image and redeemed by Jesus our Lord and Savior. We thank you that we each receive your blessing equally. Father as your children we rely on you for all good things and you never fail. Thank you for there not being disparaging treatment in your kingdom regarding your children; even here on earth when your will is not followed. In Jesus' name, we pray. Amen

Day 207

> If possible, so far as it depends on you, live peaceably
> with all. (Romans 12:18 ESV)

In his sermon on the mount Jesus said, "Blessed is the peacemakers". Peace has been broken in our lives by the influx of sin. We, God's precious people can break the bonds of chaos in our lives by following the two commands of Jesus. Love the Lord your God with all your might and love your neighbor as yourself. If we would embrace this teaching of our Lord Jesus, then the world will be a place of peace. Let peace begin with you.

Prayer: Lord God of Peace and Harmony, forgive us for our acts of aggression against one another. Guide us towards everlasting peace which is found in Christ Jesus. Help us to live at peace with all mankind. In Jesus' name we pray. Amen

Day 208

> Have you not read this Scripture: "'The stone that the builders rejected has become the cornerstone? (Mark 12:10 ESV)

Understanding the importance of the capstone in an ancient building project we see that it was the essential stone which led to the laying of a solid foundation. This stone was the guide for the laying of all other stones. Every other aspect of the building was centered on the capstone. In our lives we must seek Jesus to be the capstone on which we center our very being. Our goals, values, actions and morals should be centered on Christ Jesus, the "capstone the builders rejected".

Prayer: Lord God the foundation of our lives, hear our prayer. Father God, as the capstone is set at the inauguration of a building we want to acknowledge you as the cornerstone of our lives. You are the center of our lives and all that we could ever hope to accomplish must first be centered on you. Thank you for being that firm foundation upon which we can build. Help us to align our lives with the cornerstone of creation. In the name of Jesus, we pray. Amen

Day 209

> Cast your cares on the Lord and he will sustain you;
> he will never let the righteous fall. (Psalm 55:22 NIV)

When you place your trust in the Lord you can be assured he will hear you when you call out to him. As a Father hears the word "daddy" when his child call so the Father God hears His children. As a Father will pick up his fallen child so our father in Heaven raises us up, the fallen who are calling on His name.

Prayer: Father God, we children of men seem to care more for what this life has to offer than for what awaits us in your eternal kingdom. Forgive us for our misplaced values. Thank you for not turning your back on us as we seek after those things which will fade away. Thank you for daily provision O God our Jehovah Jireh. Help us to return to you our first love from whom all blessings flow. In Jesus' name, we pray this. Amen

Day 210

> Therefore, let us leave the elementary doctrine of Christ
> and go on to maturity, not laying again a foundation of
> repentance from dead works and of faith toward God.
> (Hebrews 6:1 ESV)

The elementary or foundational teachings regarding Christ says, "He came and died so that mankind might receive Salvation through Him". This is an elemental truth that cannot be circumvented. In knowing this there are established directives which are to be followed by the professing Christian. These directives do not lead to salvation, but they do lead to a more harmonious life while living on this earth. When you live according to the directives of our loving God, sin then is put aside as we walk in the completeness of His word as mature Christians.

Prayer: Lord God Almighty, unlike mankind who so easily get irritated with one another your patience with us seems endless. Father God in many cases we learn about you as small children yet when we arrive at adulthood we still only understand you from an elementary perspective. Forgive us for not growing and thereby having to begin over and again with the basic principles of how we are connected to you through Christ Jesus our Savior. Thank you for your mercy which endures forever. In Jesus' name, we pray. Amen

Day 211

Be angry and do not sin; do not let the sun go down on
your anger. (Ephesians 4:26 ESV)

There is nothing wrong with getting angry. Anger is a healthy emotion which allows a person to in some cases survive. Anger can be misplaced and even improperly handled. Anger which causes prolonged elevated blood pressure and heartbeat needs to be managed before it results in an unwanted action. Door slamming, punching objects and persons, screaming and storming out of a room are not proper ways of expressing your anger. Always direct anger towards the problem not towards a person.

Prayer: O God of serenity, from time to time we children of men get so angry with others that we cannot think straight. Father God not only do we get angry, but we also retain that anger for days, weeks, months and even years. Father we know your word says to not let the sun go down while we are still in our anger. Lord help us to not carry our anger over as we move into another day. In Jesus' name we pray. Amen

Day 212

Give me understanding, that I may keep your law and
observe it with my whole heart. (Psalm 119:34 ESV)

The Bible says the heart is deceitful above all things. But through understanding of our creator God we can be brought to the path of knowledge which leads to eternal life. Seek to purify your heart by displacing the worldly pursuits with spiritual truths.

Prayer: Almighty God our Father in Heaven, our knowledge of you is limited only by our inability to comprehend your will and your ways in our lives. Give us O God insight into your edicts so we may observe them with our whole mind, body and soul. In Jesus' name we pray. Amen

Day 213

let us draw near to God with a sincere heart in full
assurance of faith, having our hearts sprinkled to
cleanse us from a guilty conscience and having our
bodies washed with pure water. (Hebrews 10:22 NIV)

It takes a sincere heart to draw near to God. If your heart is deceitful
then your guilty conscience will preclude you from seeking God's
presence. Darkness cannot overcome the presence of light. When you
trust in God with your whole heart then it is easy to follow in his
footsteps. For us a faith walk begins with a pure and undefiled heart.
To begin that walk, we must first be cleansed in the waters of Baptism
and given renewal by the Holy Spirit.

Prayer: Heavenly Father God, the only thing that keeps us from an
intimate relationship with you is our own reluctance to seek cleansing,
monitoring and maintenance of our hearts. Father, it is through Christ
Jesus alone that we have a conscience free of guilt. Thank you for the
cleansing waters of Baptism which washes away our sins. Help us to be
baptized in your word daily so that we may draw near to you without
hesitation or human reservation. Hear our prayer O God in the name
of Jesus. Amen

Day 214

And whatever you do, in word or deed, do everything
in the name of the Lord Jesus, giving thanks to God the
Father through him. (Colossians 3:17 ESV)

When you invoke the validation of the Lord Jesus Christ into the
activities of your life, you will certainly operate in the glow of the
pure light of the world which is Christ Jesus. Thank God the Father
that because of the direction of the light of the world your actions are
refined into a purity which is unknown by the world.

Prayer: Lord God Almighty, as we begin each new day we lift our voices in the name of Jesus in praise to thank you. Father God as we begin every task set before us we praise you in the name of Jesus for its completion even before its beginning. LORD in all we do we give you thanks for your continued blessings in the name of Jesus which are renewed daily. And most of all in the name of Jesus we thank you for giving us life through Jesus who carried our sins to Calvary. In Jesus' name, we pray. Amen

Day 215

And we all, with unveiled face, beholding the glory of the Lord, are being transformed into the same image from one degree of glory to another. For this comes from the Lord who is the Spirit. (2 Corinthians 3:18 ESV)

Transformation into more Christ likeness is not an overnight process. God's Holy Spirit wants to reproduce in you the character of Jesus. But like a garden this process take time and is not immediate. As with the garden the seed must first be planted then germination takes place. The bud then bursts forth from the earth and eventually blossoms into the final bloom which is pleasing to the eye or good for food. We grow slowly into Christ likeness therefore be patient; allowing the Holy Spirit to accomplish his work in you.

Prayer: Lord God of Glory, as we continue to study your word, seek your presence in our daily situations and communicate with you through prayer our hope is to be transformed ever-increasing with Christ likeness in our lives. Help us Lord God to blossom into Jesus' image with ever increasing glory. In Jesus name we pray this. Amen

Day 216

For this God is our God forever and ever; he will be our guide even to the end. (Psalms 48:14 NIV)

The same God who initiated the creation by saying "Let there be" is the same God who says, "I go and prepare a place for you, I will come back and take you to be with me that you also may be where I am.". God loves his created people despite our deficiencies. He continues to pursue us as his blessed children who he desires to have live with him in a perfect place. If we allow ourselves to be sensitive to his directions, there waits for us eternal life.

O God, you are God and you are God all by yourself. Who is there like you O God? You placed the heavens and the earth in their rotation in the universe. You give life and you take life. You laid down your incarnate life that we might have eternal life. Thank you for being our Shepherd-King; watching over us from the womb to the tomb, then promising to one day return to carry us to a home with you forever. In the name of the Father, Son and Holy Spirit we pray with gratitude. Amen

Day 217

I am he that liveth, and was dead; and, behold, I am alive for evermore, Amen; and have the keys of hell and of death. (Revelation 1:18 KJV)

God took on human flesh that he might experience the ignominious death which was due to mankind. In the form of the man Jesus God dwelt among us to begin the building of his church. Through that church God was initiating the illumination which would dissipate the darkness of ignorance which mankind was embracing through his sinful acts and nature. God came as Jesus to show us the way to salvation. Follow his path to your eternity in the kingdom which he has prepared for you.

Prayer: Lord God, we know you are the God who clothed himself in human flesh to become incarnate among mankind; that you might take death as the means of redemption for those whom you love and love you. Thank you that in the man Jesus you died but three days later you became alive and now live forevermore. Thank you that through this act you have prepared for us a way to one day live forever with you in your kingdom. In Jesus' name we pray. Amen

Day 218

a false witness who pours out lies and a man who stirs
up dissension among brothers. (Proverbs 6:19 NIV)

The word hate is a strong word used to demonstrate disgust with someone or something. For the Bible to speak of God hating should be an eye opener for us. A liar who is deceiving God's people is at the top of the list of humans who can be hated by a loving God. A false lying witness does extensive damage to the kingdom building process. By lying a person causes division in the body of Christ which causes misinformation to wrongly sway brethren which brings on conflict. Avoid lying and causing discord in the kingdom.

Prayer: Holy Spirit of God, work within us the ability to travel the difficult path which is less traveled which leads to peace. Help us to share the love that is from God with each other in our daily interaction. Spirit of God give us a humble heart and lowly spirit, so we may follow the path of peace. O Lord let dissention return to the gates of hell from which it originated. This we ask in Jesus' name. Amen

Day 219

Be patient, therefore, brothers, until the coming of the
Lord. See how the farmer waits for the precious fruit
of the earth, being patient about it, until it receives the
early and the late rains. (James 5:7 ESV)

Patience has its own reward which comes from God above. If you were to see a butterfly attempting to break free of a cocoon you should wait for the process to play itself out. If you aid the butterfly you will never experience the beauty of its flight as it spreads its wings because it will die prematurely because you opened the cocoon instead of allowing the creature to break free using its God given ability. Just as undercooked food, an un-hatched egg, a premature birth, offering an opinion before knowing all the facts all of which lead to an unwholesome result. Ask God to work patience in you.

Prayer: Lord God Almighty, clothe us with patience. Do not let us be overly anxious as we await your return but let us continue in our striving to please you as we live in harmony with one another. It is better to be absent from the body and present with you but while we are still here give us the ability to wait patiently for the return of our Lord and Savior Jesus Christ. In Christ Jesus' name we pray. Amen

Day 220

> As you know, we consider blessed those who have persevered. You have heard of Job's perseverance and have seen what the Lord finally brought about. The Lord is full of compassion and mercy. (James 5:11 NIV)

We have often heard patience is a virtue, we have often heard about the people having the patience of Job. We know the Bible identifies patience as one of the fruit of the Spirit. Patience gives us the ability to tolerate the unacceptable. Patience is the precursor to perseverance. We need patience to endure so that we then have the resolve to continue amid hardship, adversity, suffering and affliction. God's love, God's mercy and God's compassion is there to carry us through the difficult time and strengthen us with patience and perseverance.

Prayer: Father God in Heaven, people speak of the patience of Job, yet it is not the patience which we ought to mention but rather his perseverance. Lord help us to carry on through the various trials we find ourselves immersed in. Give us the tenacity to move forward regardless of hindrances placed before and behind our path which are there to hold us back. Help us to set our faces in resolve to accomplish the task however insurmountable. Strengthen us Father God as you strengthened Christ for the work set before him. This we ask in Jesus' name. Amen

Day 221

> "Woe to you, scribes and Pharisees, hypocrites! For you are like whitewashed tombs, which outwardly appear beautiful, but within are full of dead people's bones and all uncleanness. (Matthew 23:27 ESV)

We take paint to add a fresh clean look to our homes, both on the interior and the exterior. Prior to the application of paint, we see smudges of grime, discoloration due to lack of cleaning or mildew from exposure to the weather. Our lives are like that house in need of a fresh coat of paint. Sin causes us to be grungy; to be stained with the ways of the world which are coated with the soot of indecent behavior. We must seek to be washed in the blood of Christ Jesus to cleanse us of all impurity. Then we must be vigilant to avoid recontamination.

Prayer: Almighty and Everlasting Father God, we seek to be real before you in all things. We do not want to be people who on the exterior look like saints but on the inside are frauds, full of decay. Help us Lord to walk the walk as we talk the talk. Lord God help us to identify the sin which indwells us so that we do not continue comparing ourselves to others. Lord this appearance driven society we live in causes us to exhibit behavior not consistent with our true nature. Lord in your mercy change our hearts and nature that they may not conflict with who you want us to be. Please hear our prayer in Jesus' name. Amen

Day 222

> Your wickedness will punish you; your backsliding will rebuke you. Consider then and realize how evil and bitter it is for you when you forsake the LORD your God and have no awe of me," declares the Lord, the LORD Almighty. (Jeremiah 2:19 NIV)

We live in a sinful and wicked world. There are assaults, rapes, murders and thefts. All those things occur because people lust after that which they do not possess. Because the love of God does not reside in the heart of people they tend to seek gratification by focusing on what makes them feel good. We cannot continue to turn our backs on God and expect to have a world where there is peace, compassion and love. All that the world offers are of a temporary nature and after the initial euphoria has worn off, we need a new infusion to bring us back to an ecstatic state. When God is our focus we can experience constant euphoria.

Prayer: Father God in Heaven, we have sinned against you because we seek with resolve those things which the world declares as important; turning our back on you our God who created heaven and the earth. Forgive us we beg you. Renew us as we appeal to you. Help us to consign you as that awesome entity of significance we seek after with our whole heart. In Jesus' name we ask this. Amen

Day 223

> ²²The iniquities of the wicked ensnare them, and they are caught in the toils of their sin. ²³They die for lack of discipline, and because of their great folly they are lost. (Proverbs 5:22-23 NRSV)

Sin brings its own punishment as the wicked soon find out. It is like stepping into two feet of mud with both feet, before you realize it you become trapped and cannot free yourself without help. For many immoralities of thought is the catalyst which leads to acting out and before you know it, like a fish on a hook you cannot break free. Ask the Holy Spirit to keep you away from wicked acts.

Prayer: Merciful Lord God, it is so very easy for us children of men to be led astray. We all allow temptation to paint us a picture which at first glance promises it will satisfy our lustful nature. What we do not see hidden behind the instant gratification is the pain for everyone touched by those people involved. Help us to avoid the snare which is set by the adversary. Help us to walk towards eternity as faithful followers of Christ and not walk towards death covered in reckless deeds. In Jesus' name, we pray this. Amen

Day 224

O LORD God of hosts, Who is mighty like You,
O LORD? Your faithfulness also surrounds You.
(Psalm 89:8 NKJV)

God is all powerful, mighty, benevolent and loving. There is none like God in Heaven and on the earth. God can be depended on because he is truth and His truth spills over into our realm when we seek His face. God is always the same awaiting your call at any time or place.

Prayer: Lord God of Hosts, we are a capricious people. We turn our affection on and off on a whim. Thank you that you O Lord God Almighty are not like us. Thank you that you are faithful in all things. Thank you that your mercies are renewed daily and we are the recipients of your grace, mercy and love in Christ Jesus. In Jesus' name, we pray. Amen

Day 225

Now it is required that those who have been given a
trust must prove faithful. (1 Cor 4:2 NIV)

This scripture speaks to anyone who would share the Gospel Message of Salvation to a hurting world. As each professing Christian is a part of the Royal Priesthood, it is incumbent that everyone realize that they are to share the message without personal wisdom as its basis. The Message is to be the pure doctrine of faith in Christ Jesus and the acceptance of salvation which was offered from the Cross.

Prayer: Father God in Heaven give us the spirit of faithfulness. Lord God do not let us be wishy-washy in our lives as we proclaim we are followers of Christ. Lord we do not want to be found straddling the fence. Help us to stand firm as children of the living God and faithful servants to the WORD. In Jesus' name we pray. Amen

Day 226

> In overflowing anger for a moment I hid my face from
> you, but with everlasting love I will have compassion on
> you," says the Lord, your Redeemer. (Isaiah 54:8 ESV)

What a wonderful, compassionate God of love we have. If God gave us what we truly deserved, we would all be lost engrossed in our sin. The Bible speaks of how God was grieved in his heart that he created mankind, and therefore he destroyed all life on the earth with a flood. God loves us through our sinful nature and because of that he will never turn his back on us. We on the other hand, frequently turn away from God to pursue sinful desires, then when we get found out we run back to God for solace.

Prayer: Lord God our Redeemer, only once did you hide your face from mankind for a portion of time. This happened during the days of Noah when you brought the flood to wash the earth clean of the corruption mankind brought about. Since that day you have given us everlasting kindness and compassion. Thank you, LORD, for redeeming us through your son Christ Jesus. Thank you for not seeing us as the sinners we are but seeing us as the righteousness that Christ makes us. In Jesus' name we pray. Amen

Day 227

> The god of this age has blinded the minds of unbelievers,
> so that they cannot see the light of the gospel of the
> glory of Christ, who is the image of God. (2 Cor 4:4 NIV)

The god of this world is Satan. He travels back and forth about the earth seeking those who he can influence, use, devour or kill. There are spiritually weak people who inhabit this earth whose minds are blind to the truth of God's divine word yet receive the doctrine of men as gospel truth. All who reject the truth of God's precious word fall victim to the tricks of the devil and all his deception. We must open blinded eyes to see and have revealed to us the true pure light of God's word which illuminates our path. Receive that word as a light to your path and a lamp to guide your feet.

Prayer: Lord God of the Gospel, many people on this earth are blinded to the message of salvation found in Christ Jesus. Father God open blinded eyes that your created people may see, understand and believe. Let the light of the gospel and the glories of Christ overcome the darkness and ignorance. Illuminate that deception which has been cast upon many people in this world by the god of this world, so it may dissipate. Lord in your mercy, hear our prayer. This we ask in Jesus' name. Amen

Day 228

Be kind to one another, tenderhearted, forgiving one another, as God in Christ forgave you. (Ephesians 4:32 ESV)

We live in a world of confusion. When there are moments of serenity we sometimes reflect on past activity in which we participated, and we are not proud of how we handled some of those situations. In many cases it is because we did not act out in love, with compassion and a spirit of forgiveness was not present. We are a social people. To cohabitate with others of our species we must be loving and lovable, which results in kindness, tenderheartedness and forgiveness. These qualities are taught to our hearts by the word of God. Let us live them.

Prayer: Lord God of Love, we children of men tend to act with hostility towards each other in this dark world. Father this is not your desire for your children. Lord God you speak to us saying to "love one another", "be kind to one another" and "forgive one another". Lord by the power of your Holy Spirit, please write these words in our hearts that we can live by them and make this a better place while we dwell here. Father hear our prayer we ask in Jesus' name. Amen

Day 229

Whom have I in heaven but you? And there is nothing on earth that I desire besides you. (Psalm 73:25 ESV)

The earth filled with its precious stones and precious metals seduce mankind to seek them as the most valuable thing in the world. The glitter and the glitz resemble the brass carousel ring which is sought on this merry-go-round called life. Also, people want to know and rub elbows with celebrities of this world thinking that makes them more acceptable to other people. We should desire to have a relationship with our creator God because nothing in Heaven or on earth is more important.

Prayer: Heavenly father God, we have parents, siblings, spouses, friends and acquaintances but each of them at any time could turn their backs on us. Not so with you Lord God. Lord there is nothing and no one more desirable than you. Lord there is no one more faithful than you. Father, thank you for being unmovable, unshakable and steadfast each, and every day. In Jesus' name, we pray. Amen

Day 230

⁴But God, who is rich in mercy, because of His great love with which He loved us, ⁵even when we were dead in trespasses, made us alive together with Christ (by grace you have been saved). (Ephesians 2:4-5 NKJV)

Like the air we breathe, so too are we immersed in the sinful activities of the flesh. We sin in thought, word and deed and no matter how hard we try we cannot separate ourselves from sins clutches. Thankfully we serve a merciful God who knows our failing yet does not offer us justice which deserves punishment but instead gives us grace with its undeserved clemency.

Prayer: Father God, we are forever grateful for the love you have for us. Although we are unworthy it is by your grace through Christ that you have made us your children. Through Christ Jesus we are eternally secure although we were once dead but through him we are now alive. Thank you, Lord. By the name of Jesus, we pray. Amen

Day 231

> Therefore, my beloved, as you have always obeyed, so now, not only as in my presence but much more in my absence, work out your own salvation with fear and trembling. (Philippians2:12 ESV)

Salvation is a continual process for the believer. This ongoing work is not a reference to salvation gained through the efforts of mankind. But it refers to the involvement of a single-minded purpose. This purpose expresses itself through reverence to God through Christ Jesus and love for mankind as Jesus has commanded.

Prayer: Lord God of grace, often people think that because of the world we live in which gives nothing for free they must pay a price to obtain salvation. In society today, Lord God people think that it is by the works of their hands that salvation comes. Heavenly Father we declare today knowing in our hearts salvation comes through no other means but through our Lord and Savior Jesus Christ. Father God, thank you for Christ's death and resurrection that we might be given eternal life through him. In Jesus' name, we pray. Amen

Day 232

> [18]For the wrath of God is revealed from heaven against all ungodliness and unrighteousness of men, who suppress the truth in unrighteousness, [19]because what

may be known of God is manifest in them, for God has
shown it to them. (Romans 1:18-19 NKJV)

How often do we say we are Christian to people we meet? But does
our action validate our words. Does our action reflect what we are
saying to those around us? This is especially true where forgiveness
is a directive given to the Christian. Because of continued human
dysfunction which causes distrust we become cynical. "Nobody can
be trusted", we think. We view everyone under the magnifying glass
to scrutinize their every action. And in so doing we will of course find
fault. But I challenge you to look in the mirror. How much honesty do
you see there? God has the right to be cynical with us, but he does not.
Ask him to help you not be so with others.

Prayer: Lord God Creator of Heaven and Earth, thank you, that you are
patient with us. In wrath you could dispense with us for our foolish
ways. Yet you O God in love look at us and see your son Jesus who for
our sakes died for us. Help us Father God to walk upright; forgive us
our sins. Help us to live with the sole purpose of being more Christ like
each day. Father in Jesus' name we pray. Amen

Day 233

But the Lord was with Joseph and showed him steadfast
love and gave him favor in the sight of the keeper of the
prison. (Genesis 39:21 ESV)

God's favor can change the most difficult of circumstances and cause
people to grant you kindness where it is not anticipated. Within the
walls of a prison God can cause favor to fall on his chosen people.
When you see a person receiving something other humans think
should not be, that could be tangible evidence that God has sanctioned
and supported that person.

Prayer: Father God, we often find ourselves looking up from the
bottom of an abyss. Lord your children find themselves in the bottom

of financial, relational, health or career pits. Almighty Father in some of those situations you are molding us to conform to what you desire for us. In each of those situations it always looks like we are left alone in the pit, but you are there. Father help your people to know that you remain right beside them in every location in which they find themselves, whether it is on top of the mountain or down in the valley. Father we pray with gratitude through Christ Jesus. Amen

Day 234

To each is given the manifestation of the Spirit for the common good. (1 Corinthians 12:7 ESV)

The Holy Spirit imparts abilities on individuals with the sole purpose of those talents being given and used for the benefit of the church. Remember the church is the total body of believers, not just those within the walls of the building where you worship.

Prayer: Almighty and Everlasting God, you gift individuals as you determine. Some are teachers, preachers, prayers, servers, cleaners and so on. LORD you give us each something to use in the kingdom for your purpose. Make your people to understand that each gifting is not for self-profit but for the benefit of all. As we then share our gifts with others we become the body of Christ which works for the common good of all. Father God, work in our hearts the spirit of understanding which will enable us to walk in this truth. In Jesus' Holy name we pray. Amen

Day 235

My little children, I am writing these things to you so that you may not sin. But if anyone does sin, we have an advocate with the Father, Jesus Christ the righteous. (1 John 2:1 ESV)

Without God's grace we would be lost to an eternity of living in the pit, which has been prepared for lost souls who have followed the adversary. But for those who look to the light of God's Word, which is Christ Jesus he bestows grace, unmerited grace which gives us hope in our struggles with correct living. In our daily walk we seek to be more Christ like in thought, word and deed. When we find ourselves operating outside of that mode we can then seek forgiveness by confessing our sin. God no longer sees the sin but only one of his children who have faith in Christ as their savior. It is wonderful that God with us stands between heaven and earth as our advocate.

Prayer: Gracious Lord God our Father, we would be lost if it were not for your unlimited grace. Thank you that although we constantly fall short of the mark, your grace is there to give us hope and guide us from the path of despair. Father with this awareness of hope which is found in your grace through Christ Jesus redirect our actions, words and thoughts that we may give you glory in all we say think and do. Lord help us to accomplish this as a demonstration of our love for you and your grace. Through Christ Jesus we pray. Amen

Day 236

> No, in all these things we are more than conquerors
> through him who loved us. (Romans 8:37 NIV)

In ancient times a conqueror defeated cities, kingdoms and civilizations through means of combative effort. Walled cities were laid siege to for years at a time. This happened, until through depletion of warriors by combat, starvation or thirst because of a lack of water caused the besieged to surrender and be taken captive. In some cases, the warrior who laid siege were overcome and defeated and either surrendered or were devastated through combat. The conqueror was then considered victorious and the battle was his. Mankind has been in conflict since the fall of man in the Garden of Eden. God said that he would defeat the originator of sin through the seed of the woman who he deceived. Because of God's unyielding love for us, we have conquered sin through faith in Christ Jesus.

Prayer: Heavenly Father God, you give us all things. Father God you love us with an unconditional love that is beyond our human understanding. Empower us to love one another with that same fervor. Lord God Almighty your greatest act of love was that you clothed yourself in human flesh and came as the man Jesus to live among us. You came to love us. And you came to die for us. What greater love is there than this. Thank you. Help us to conquer our limitations that we may grow more Christ like each day. Father we pray in the name of the Father, Son and Holy Spirit. Amen

Day 237

> But exhort one another every day, as long as it is called "today," that none of you may be hardened by the deceitfulness of sin. (Hebrews 3:13 ESV)

Have you ever asked someone to do something for you and they told you "I can't do it today, I'll try and get to it tomorrow"? what they are saying is this, "I don't want to commit my time now to what you want of me". Why is that? Because there is no such day as tomorrow. There is only yesterday and today. The day after today when it arrives will again be today. Tomorrow is an illusion. We are to encourage one another in spiritual matters today, which is now. Never put it off or it may not be done. Tomorrow is a lie that is not sustainable. If Jesus had said on that faithful Friday let me wait until tomorrow, where would we be? Live and love in today.

Prayer: Almighty and Everlasting Father God, thank you for today. Forgive us if we did not live yesterday as you intended. Help us with our sinful shortcomings. Help us to encourage one another to live as you desire us to live; that is as your children loving and caring for one another. Father in the name of Jesus, protect us from the deceitfulness of sin as we travel through this life. In Jesus' name, we pray. Amen

Day 238

Where there is no revelation, the people cast off restraint; But happy is he who keeps the law. (Proverbs 29:18 NKJV)

Keeping our eye on God through the study of His word leads to a fulfilling, happy life. Through study we obtain a prophetic word to share with a sin sick, dying world. When the word of life is shared, people turn from perishing to life through Christ Jesus. That farseeing word must be proclaimed; people must be given an opportunity to hear, receive and learn from that word. If the word is not given people have an opportunity to keep the law but keeping the law is impossible for sinful humans.

Prayer: Lord God our Father in Heaven, Father God open the eyes of your people that they may see the restraints imposed upon us as we wallow in sin. Lord impress the vision of salvation into our hearts and souls so that we do not perish. Lord allow this to come to your people as an illuminating revelation from which they never turn back to the sightlessness of lack of vision. In Jesus' name, we pray. Amen

Day 239

And he said, "My presence will go with you, and I will give you rest." (Exodus 33:14 NKJV)

As a child of God, it is vitally important to remember God is always present, even when you do not think so. God never sleeps; he is your constant companion. Jesus has said I am with you always even to the end of the age. For us, rest is that land of Milk and Honey Jesus has prepared so that we may be where He is. He is with us now spiritually but will return physically to carry us to that prepared place for prepared people.

Prayer: Lord God of Comfort, in this world of turmoil it is only through our relationship with you that we find peace. Thank you that because of our Lord and Savior Jesus Christ we have the comfort of your continual presence. Thank you, Father God for the rest that your presence provides in the lives of those who trust in the Lord. Through Jesus our Prince of Peace we pray. Amen

Day 240

> Owe no one anything, except to love each other,
> for the one who loves another has fulfilled the law.
> (Romans 13:8 ESV)

In this life, we owe our very existence to a Loving, Caring and Merciful God. To Him we owe everything and to demonstrate our Love to Him is to carry out His commands. His greatest command was that we love one another with an unconditional agape love which demands nothing in return.

Prayer: Lord God of Love, your word says to owe no one anything except love. Forgive us as our affections for one another are cooled by self-interests, pride, lust and greed. Help us Lord in our detestable state which hinders us from loving one another as you have loved us. Lord hear our prayer in Jesus' name as we seek to pay our debt of love, one to another. Amen

Day 241

> For the thing that I fear comes upon me, and what I
> dread befalls me. (Job 3:25 ESV)

Like Job many people today are in fear of a great calamity befalling them. For some people, it is the fear of cancer or some other terminal illness. Many wealthy people who have always had plenty their greatest fear is penury. For people who have had a lifelong partner it is loneliness. People who live tranquil and secure lives fear that lifestyle being broken. Remember in all things for those who Love God things are being worked out for their good, and God has not given you a spirit of fear. So, standup, straighten your back and look to God.

Prayer: Lord God our Mighty God, our protector. Thank you, Lord, for placing a hedge of protection around us to keep the enemy at a distance. Lord there are times when he gets through and inflicts upon us his diseases of anxiety, deceit, waning faith and any other tactic he can steer onto our path to cause us to doubt your love for us. You Lord are faithful and trustworthy as illustrated by the cross of Christ. When what we dread comes upon us you remind us in your word that you are always with us even to the end. In Jesus' name, we pray. Amen

Day 242

I press on toward the goal for the prize of the upward
call of God in Christ Jesus. (Philippians3:14 ESV)

In track and field events where the contestants run, there is a beginning point and end objective in the race. As children of God our beginning was in the womb and many thinks that their ending is in the tomb. That is not so. For the Christian, the goal or end of the race is our heavenly home with our Lord and Savior Jesus Christ. Therefore, place your faith in Jesus as Lord and Savior then salvation in His Heavenly Kingdom is yours. Make Heaven your goal and press on!

Prayer: O Great and all powerful I AM, you have endowed each person with potential. Help us Lord to hone that potential so that we become focused in our calling to join you in your kingdom building work. It is only through your enablement that we can excel in the work of delivering the message to those who are not yet a part of the body of Christ. Help us O God to press on In Jesus' name, we pray. Amen

Day 243

He is the Rock, his work is perfect: for all his ways are
judgment: a God of truth and without iniquity, just and
right is he. (Deuteronomy 32:4 KJV)

Like quartz and granite which are of the hardest rocks known to man God is solid as a rock. Like rock God is stable and permanent. We His children find our stability as we rest on Him for our daily living and cling to Him for support. Our God is faithful and trustworthy as he deals with us in a fair and equitable manner.

Prayer: Eternal God of fidelity, in you O Lord there is no deceit. Unlike common man whose character embraces deception, you O God can be relied on. Lord we do not always lie to manipulate, deceive or harm. Father there are lies which are spoken to not offend, to not cause inconvenience and to not cause undue pain. Save us, O Lord, from lying lips and from deceitful tongues, even when done with good in mind as the resulting end. Father we pray this through Jesus, the truth. Amen

Day 244

> For this reason, I also suffer these things; nevertheless
> I am not ashamed, for I know whom I have believed
> and am persuaded that He is able to keep what I have
> committed to Him until that Day. (2 Tim. 1:12 NKJV)

Throughout the world, Christians are being persecuted for their belief in Jesus Christ. As the Apostles suffered and rejoiced over that suffering of persecution we too ought to rejoice. Persecutions comes because of the devil knowing his time is short. Because his time is short he wants to distract you, disillusion you and intimidate you with threats and brutality. Know this, Jesus has authority over your eternal soul and the devil cannot touch it.

Prayer: Lord God our Stronghold, we are under constant attack by the enemy. Father as we are continually bombarded by life's pressures. Doubts sometimes arise that you have abandoned us. The enemy uses this doubt urging us to raise questions such as "if I am saved why then does God allow me these problems"? Lord Jesus help us as we pray saying we place our trust in you. Lord no matter how dark the days ahead may seem we know there is the Sunlight of the Son waiting to pierce the darkness and guide us through into his marvelous light. Lord help us in our moments of weakness. In Jesus' name, we pray. Amen

Day 245

Come to me, all who labor and are heavy laden, and I will give you rest. (Matthew 11:28 NKJV)

Life and its many challenges over the years begin to take a toll on every human being under the sun. Illness, finances, relationships, school, jobs, disasters, their aftermath and other responsibilities make us feel like the mythological character Atlas who bore the weight of the sky on his shoulders. When you feel burdened turn to the comfort of Jesus the only one who can give us rest in dealing with the troubles of this life. He says to us come to him for rest from the world's burdens. Turn it over to Jesus he is your burden bearer and your heavy load sharer.

Prayer: God of comfort, in this world of turmoil and commotion we become overworked, under relaxed and unable to unwind. Lord even as we lay down to sleep our minds race with the events of the day and we are pondering the purposed events of the next day. Forgive us for not following your example to take a Sabbath rest. Thank you for saying come to you all who are heavy laden, and you will give rest. Lord we would be lost without you. Hear our prayer in Jesus' name. Amen

Day 246

And he did not permit him but said to him, "Go home to your friends and tell them how much the Lord has done for you, and how he has had mercy on you." (Mark 5:19 ESV)

We all have experienced a test as we traversed through this life. Keep in mind our test results in our testimony. When God has carried you through a trying, tumultuous situation, you want to tell somebody about the goodness of the Lord. When you know in your heart that you should be dead laying in your grave headed for a burning hell, yet God has changed your life and brought you from the outhouse to the penthouse, you want to tell somebody. Share what Jesus has done for you.

Prayer: Merciful and Matchless Father God our Creator, you have given each of us the commission to go and tell the Good News of what you have accomplished in our lives through Christ Jesus. Lord you have saved us from a burning hell by the unselfish act of love illustrated by Jesus carrying our sins to the cross of Calvary. O God remove the spirits of shyness, apprehension, shame, doubt or lack of confidence so we may carry the message of your salvation to those who have not yet been caressed by the healing touch of Jesus our Lord and Savior. In Jesus' name, we pray. Amen

Day 247

for all have sinned and fall short of the glory of God.
(Romans 3:23 NIV)

Sin, you live with it every hour of every waking day; there is no avoiding it. Our thoughts lead us to sin. Our eyes lead us to sin. Our mouths emit sinful words which are stored up in our hearts. Every man, woman, boy and girl has a sin problem. If anyone should say he was once a sinner and now is not, run as fast as you can and get away from him because the truth is not in him. Because we cannot rid ourselves of our sinful nature, we should with grateful hearts thank our redeeming God for the grace given through Christ Jesus' sacrifice on our behalf. Despite sin, because of Jesus we are now made right with God if we accept Jesus as Lord and Savior knowing that God raised him from the dead for us.

Prayer: Merciful God our Father, we have all fallen short and sinned by what we have done and what we have left undone. Thank you for continually cleaning our slate and giving each of us another chance.

Thank you, Lord God that you no longer remember our sin as we come to you through Christ Jesus with a repentant heart. Thank you that your mercies are renewed each day. In Jesus' name, we pray. Amen

Day 248

> O taste and see that the Lord is good: blessed is the
> man that trusts in him. (Psalm 34:8 NKJV)

Many times, people look at a drug addict or alcoholic and say things like: "I don't want that person anywhere near me". Particularly for the addicted people, some look at them as thieves and in many cases unless they are employed they very well might be. But what about the ones that God has changed to be men and women of God? Those same drug addict and alcoholics when touched by the love of God can become on fire for the Lord, seeking to tell others how good the Lord is. God is good, all the time and all the time God is Good! God changes hearts through Jesus. So, accept that.

Prayer: Merciful and Gracious Lord God, we children of men have selective tastes in our food, activities, companionship, religion and methods of worship. Father God our taste in music as it relates to religion is diverse. The type of building we want to worship in is varied. Our method of prayer is assorted. Father we even look at each other in our differences with a disparaging eye. Merciful and Loving God our Father help us to move closer to you and know you in your fullness. Help us to taste of the grace, mercy, love and kindness which you wait to share with each of us. Father let us all know you in the singleness of purpose found in Christ Jesus, which leads us to salvation. In Jesus' name, we pray. Amen

Day 249

> Joseph called the name of the firstborn Manasseh.
> "For," he said, "God has made me forget all my hardship
> and all my father's house." (Genesis 41:51 ESV)

Toil and trouble is the plight of every human born of a woman. There is however something that is amazing. When your mind is on the goodness of God those things pale in comparison. Trouble does not last always, it is only for a season. God, if asked will impart through His Holy spirit forgetfulness and the past will be forgotten. Ask Him and see for yourself.

Prayer: Merciful and Mighty God our Father, you care for us however overbearing the burdens life places upon us. It is because of you we can approach each new day with confidence that no matter what we are confronted with we have your compassion, power, might and mercy to sustain us through the tough times. Help us to feel your presence O God in your entirety. This we pray in the name of the Father the Son and the Holy Spirit. Amen

Day 250

> But I call to God, and the Lord will save me. (Psalm 55:16 ESV)

If you believe in the words of the Bible, then you must without a doubt trust in the Lord. On this you cannot straddle the fence. If you pray and ask His protection, then believe it. If you are not going to believe it, then do not pray for it.

Prayer: Merciful Savior, in our distress you have given us the benefit of being able to call on your Holy Name. Thank you, Merciful Lord for saving us in the present and thank you for saving us for eternity to come. In Jesus' name, we pray. Amen

Day 251

> Let all that you do be done in love. (1 Corinthians 16:14 ESV)

Love should be the dominant motivator in our interaction with one another. When we conduct our activities in love towards God, others and ourselves we can only achieve an outcome which promotes concord. Anything short of love incubates strife, rivalry and conflict. Love endures all things through to an end which is mutually beneficial to all involved. Love never fails regardless of the situation because love is of God and God is love.

Prayer: Lord God Almighty, you did not create your people to hate. Therefore Lord, help us to understand that nothing that ever happens should give birth to hatred. Father God, Our Lord and Savior Jesus Christ suffered due to hatred. Help us to choose love in every situation O God that we may bring you honor in all that we say and do. This we ask in Jesus' name. Amen

Day 252

Man that is born of a woman is of few days, and full of trouble. (Job 14:1 NKJV)

If we were to live to be 100 years old, we would only live 36,525 days. This is not a long time in the scheme of things. Around us we see trees which have lived for several hundred years yet they have not yet reached maturity. The first man and woman lived many hundreds of years in the trouble they brought upon themselves. Because of the brokenness of this world we will experience trouble from birth to the grave. Despite the trouble, focus on the faithfulness of Christ, who like us experience trouble in this world. Trouble won't last always.

Prayer: Lord God Almighty, we live in a world of trouble laden with perils brought on by those who allow themselves to be used by our adversary Satan. Although we experience this daily our greatest danger is found in conceding our faith in Christ Jesus. Help us to remain strong in our faith as we traverse through the barrage of troubles this world presents to us. Lord, order our steps, actions and thoughts in your word. In Jesus' name we pray. Amen

Day 253

Teach me your way, O Lord, and I will walk in your
truth; give me an undivided heart, that I may fear your
name. (Psalm 86:11 NIV)

The Christian says in his heart "Lord come by here and dwell with
me". We ask the Lord to come and teach us his ways and make his will
"known" to us. We are a wayward people in need of God's constant
guidance. On our own we stray from the path of righteousness and
become bogged down in the sin which seeks to drag us under. Without
God we pursue artificial worships with a heart divided between the
divine and the earthly. Only God alone through Christ Jesus can turn
our hearts back to him. Let us seek him out daily asking that he teach
us heavenly truths so that we release our hold on this world and reach
wholeheartedly for, that which is above in the divine heavenly realm.

Prayer: Lord God Almighty, as we come to you in our weakness asking
you to direct us through life's challenges, we do so halfheartedly. We
approach you O God with one open hand asking for help yet clinging
to worldly matters and self-directed solutions with the other hand.
Lord God help us to clear our minds of the distractions of this world
and place our whole trust in you. Father God help us to offer not just a
part but our whole heart to you daily. This we ask in Jesus' name. Amen

Day 254

James, a servant of God and of the Lord Jesus Christ, to
the twelve tribes which are scattered abroad, greeting.
(James 1:1 NIV)

We are servants of God and should be servants to one another. We do
not exist for ourselves alone. Mankind exists to aid and support one
another. For this reason, we are to die to self and sincerely and freely
serve others. We must interact with others in a method pleasing to the
Lord and not in judging the strong or demeaning the weak. From Jesus'

authority as resurrected Lord He bids us live in harmony with one another, then each of us not in his own sufficiency, but in the sufficiency of the power of God's Holy Spirit can relinquish self-serving attitudes and offer service to one another, the church and Christ Jesus our God.

Prayer: Lord God Almighty, we your handmade servants ask your forgiveness for turning our backs on those we in our narrow thinking say are lost. Father God the truth is we would all be lost if it were not for the sacrificial suffering and death of our Lord and Savior Jesus Christ. Thank you for the resurrection which gives us hope for eternity with our Lord. Help us to not give up praying for those who need to come to faith in Christ Jesus, so they too can share eternity with all who place their faith in Christ. In Jesus' name we pray. Amen

Day 255

Count it all joy, my brothers, when you meet trials of various kinds. (James 1:2 ESV)

It has been said that there are two certainties in this life, taxes and death. I challenge that adage and add another to it. There will always be on this earth taxes, death and trouble. As God's children we have our relationship rooted in the one who created us because we can stand on his promises of redemption from the inner trials of sin which persistently invade our lives. Sin troubles mankind in every situation even in the attempted good that man seeks to accomplish. There is the taint of sin's trials in his efforts. Temptation and trials are synonymous but in them we have the promise of God's grace for the repentant sinner whose faith is in Christ Jesus.

Prayer: Lord God Almighty, it is always easier to tell someone else that they should turn their trials and troubles over to you then it is to practice this ourselves. Lord when cancer is eating away at the body. Lord when illness becomes debilitating. Lord when children, spouses, coworkers, friends or acquaintances become disagreeable, rude, vindictive or evil help us to hear "turn it over to the Lord". Lord, help us to rejoice in the midst of our trials because this is the time when we have opportunity to see you at work in our lives. Lord the outcome will draw us closer to you when we have a relationship with you no matter what happens. Thank you, Lord in the name of Jesus we pray. Amen

Day 256

(Psalm 61:8 KJV) So will I sing praise unto thy name for ever, that I may daily perform my vows.

We were created for praise. The Lord God Almighty took five days to create the earth and all that was on it then he created mankind. As man took his first breath and looked around what wonders did he see? There was the sun, sky, the earth and the fullness there of. But even more than that there was the one who created him, there was God standing before man in all his glory. As man stood before God all he probably could do was lift his hands in praise for him who created all things and all things that God had made were good. Praise to our God.

Prayer: Almighty and Everlasting Father God, we offer up prayer with hearts of expectancy. We look back on our past and see your fulfillment of our prayers and we praise you for them. Thank you, Father God for blessings, for mercy and for grace. Thank you most of all for Jesus, the fulfillment of all that we could ever ask. In Jesus' name we pray. Amen

Day 257

Oh, the depth of the riches and wisdom and knowledge of God! How unsearchable are his judgments and how inscrutable his ways! (Romans 11:33 ESV)

God is beyond understanding. And the truth of the matter is we need not understand God we need only trust Him. You cannot understand someone as mysterious as God. In our humanness, we cannot understand how a Holy God can love an unholy sinner like us. Even in our sin He uses that for His purpose.

Prayer: Almighty God our Heavenly Father, we children of men would like to think ourselves as having wisdom. Forgive us for our vanity because in you our wisdom is sinful and disobedient. Father God only wisdom which proceeds from you is of any value. Help us O God to seek after and operate in wisdom inspired by you and not the self-seeking wisdom of mankind. Lord we ask you to hear our prayer in the name of Jesus. Amen

Day 258

> Know this, my beloved brothers: let every person
> be quick to hear, slow to speak, slow to anger.
> (James 1:19 ESV)

God gave to each individual one mouth and two ears. This indicates that we should listen twice as much as we speak. Unfortunately, we tend to speak twice as much as we listen. It is often out of the necessity to be heard that we let our mouths give way to prudence in our dialogue with one another. It is sometimes better to keep our mouths shut and let people think us a fool than to open our mouths and remove all doubt.

Prayer: Lord God Almighty, we are often in conversation with our fellow human beings but how often do we intentionally listen to the other person? Father God we are people who feel we must be heard. For us the other person must listen to what we are saying because it is important. O God how foolish is the person who resorts to this type of communication. Help us to be slow to speak O God help us to be eager to listen. Father help us to listen to others since you may very well use that person to speak to us. Father God we ask this in Jesus' name Amen

Day 259

> We proclaim him, admonishing and teaching everyone
> with all wisdom, so that we may present everyone
> perfect in Christ. (Colossians 1:28 NIV)

We who call ourselves Christians are to proclaim the name of Jesus and teach of his enduring and long-suffering love. We teach of this love through our faith in him. We can share the numerous blessings of our individual relationship with God through Christ Jesus. People can typically teach what they know and when you know of the goodness of Christ it then becomes an easy assignment. We each have a message to share. First meditate on the goodness of God in your life. Next carry that message to those who have not yet acknowledged Christ as the head of their lives.

Prayer: Heavenly Father God, we seek your forgiveness in the name of Jesus for not boldly speaking the good news of salvation to those who do not know Christ Jesus as their Lord and Savior. Help us O God to warn of the impending eternal doom of dying without placing our faith in Christ as our redeemer. Lord, give us wisdom to share the message of your grace through Christ Jesus to those who are lost. In Jesus' name we pray this. Amen

Day 260

Be angry and do not sin; do not let the sun go down on your anger. (Ephesians 4:26 ESV)

Anger is one emotion which can cause severe separation between people. Anger can be easily misplaced for the Christian who seeks to walk in the will of God. We become angry with people for actions they have initiated towards us. But the Bible is clear on this one thing that the problem is not a problem of a carnal nature but of a spiritual nature. This emotion is not removed from us as we come to Christ but as in all things we are to make this emotion obedient to Christ. For the Christian is taught that his anger should not spill over into the next day. Seek to immediately resolve an issue which incites you to anger.

Prayer: Father God in Heaven, we your hand made servants can fall into a rage instantly. Lord we lose our serenity in the blink of an eye over inconsequential matters. Lord as we deal with one another help us to do so with gentleness, compassion and love. Let us not sin in our anger. O God send the Holy Spirit to empower us to fight sinful anger and cultivate peace and harmony. This we pray in Jesus' name. Amen

Day 261

> because judgment without mercy will be shown to anyone who has not been merciful. Mercy triumphs over judgment! (James 2:13 NIV)

Were you ever the go to person in a situation that called for someone to be assessed or rated? It is interesting that when that kind of authority is given to certain people they tend to sift through the individual's life with a fine-tooth comb. God has called us to be merciful in judging our peers. We must always remember that with the same severity of judgement we judge others, we shall also be judged in a like harsh manner. If we judge with mercy we shall receive mercy in our judgement.

Prayer: Merciful God our Father, forgive us O God, for not extending mercy to those who have betrayed, wronged or let us down. Father God help us to understand the magnitude of your mercy so that we can emulate you and tender mercy to one another. Father in Jesus' name we pray. Amen

Day 262

> But stay awake at all times, praying that you may have strength to escape all these things that are going to take place, and to stand before the Son of Man. (Luke 21:36 ESV)

Jesus has told us in His word that the end time is approaching; today it is closer than it was yesterday so know it is coming. We are to be aware and prayerfully in contact with our redeemer God as the day approaches. In our prayers, we should ask for the strength to endure what makes its way into our lives. Do not let the seductions of this life draw you into an apathetic attitude towards God and His day. Be steadfast and strong in the knowledge of God and nurture a deepening relationship with Him so when the day does arrive you will be found worthy to stand in the presence of the Lord.

Prayer: Almighty and Everlasting Father God, today brings us closer to the return of our Lord and Savior Jesus Christ. Father God as we wait there are many who are weighed down with deceit, anxiety, over indulgence and backsliding. Lord, for those who see the day approaching and realize that only through Christ will any be saved, help them to deliver the message of hope. Help those who hear place their strength in Christ to escape from the world and be able to stand before Christ on that faithful day when he comes. Lord, hear our prayer in Jesus' name. Amen

Day 263

Every way of a man is right in his own eyes, but the
Lord weighs the heart. (Proverbs 21:2 ESV)

For most of us we think nothing is wrong with the way we do things. And then there are those who think it is their way or you can hit the highway. Even for the person who is doing the wrong thing if you comment you might be reprimanded with "mind your own business". As life continues its course we will have opportunity to do things in a manner which pleases us, in our own way. There will be times because of being under the supervision of another we will be subjected to doing things that person's way. Whether our way or another's way God views the heart of each and we will eventually stand and answer to Him. Therefore, let us do all things God's way.

Prayer: O Lord our Omniscient God, we approach you Lord in the name of Jesus asking your forgiveness as fallen sinners. Lord we do things which seem right in our own eyes but in truth we are brick throwers who hide our hands. Father God remove anything within our hearts which is in opposition to having a clean heart which can serve you. Lord, make us more Christ like daily. We thank you Lord for illuminating the darkness and filling us with your marvelous light. In Jesus' name, we pray. Amen

Day 264

Enter by the narrow gate. For the gate is wide and the way is easy that leads to destruction, and those who enter by it are many. (Matthew 7:13 ESV)

There are one of two roads through which the travelers of this life will traverse. There is the wide road which is filled with many people. This is the popular path with all the glitz and glitter and bling to attract your attention. This great avenue has people walking shoulder to shoulder along its path crowding one another by the immense numbers there. Little do many realize that this road leads to a destructive end. There is a lesser traveled path where you occasionally find a solitary traveler steadily moving along towards its end. This is not the great highway that people tread. This narrow path must be carefully negotiated because there are pitfalls along the way which will cause you to stumble. Diligence and wisdom is needed to travel the narrow path which ends in life. The broad crowded thoroughfare or the empty narrow alleyway which seems desolate and deserted, you choose.

Prayer: Lord God Almighty, there are many times when we who profess Christianity stand-by and allow our brothers and sisters to continue down the wide path which leads to destruction. Father God we do this when we hear them speak the Lord's name in vain. Father God we do this as we see them abuse family and friends, co-worker's and peers and self. Father we do this as we see them acting out with misdeeds of immorality, wicked behavior, slander, gossip, arrogance and countless other acts which are not in alignment with your word. Father God forgive us who have stood silently by. Help us to proclaim the name of Jesus to those who are of this world and headed for destruction. This we pray in Jesus' name. Amen

Day 264

Open my eyes, that I may behold wondrous things out
of your law. (Psalm 119:18 ESV)

When we look at the words wondrous things we think of the things
God has done in our lives as a demonstration of his continued blessings
on mankind. When we hear the word law we drawback thinking of
regulations and restrictions placed on us. In God's law, there is not so
much restriction as there is peace. As we consider God's law we find
it teaches us how to live in harmony with God and one another. Only
those who revel in sin would not wish their eyes and understanding
to be opened to the knowledge of God's law.

Prayer: Heavenly Father God, in your word we find law and gospel.
Lord God we break your laws daily by sins of commission and by sins
of omission; we know sin leads to death, forgive us. Thank you for your
love displayed through the gospel which leads to eternal life, found in
Christ Jesus. Open our eyes O God to see the redeeming acts of your
love in our lives as we seek to live according to your decrees. Lord, hear
our prayer in the name of Jesus. Amen

Day 266

⁹So then, there remains a Sabbath rest for the
people of God, ¹⁰for whoever has entered God's rest
has also rested from his works as God did from his.
(Hebrews 4:9-10 ESV)

We hear of the Sabbath rest and think of taking a day off from our
labors to give our body a well-deserved rest. God in his infinite wisdom
has instore for those who faith is in Christ Jesus a sabbath rest for
both body and soul. Jesus has awaiting those who are his, an eternal
rest in him whose finished work of the cross affords them this unique
opportunity for all eternity.

Prayer: Holy and faithful Father God, you have called us to a Sabbath rest. Help us Lord God to take the time to give our bodies the rest it desires from the stressors of this life. Help us to enter, into your eternal rest and rest from our works Father God as you did when your work was completed. This we ask in the name of Jesus, through whom we will receive eternal rest. Amen

Day 267

Therefore, confess your sins to one another and pray
for one another, that you may be healed. The prayer of
a righteous person has great power as it is working.
(James 5:16 ESV)

In a certain religious denomination, there is a private confession between penitent and cleric, nowhere is scripture is this supported. What is said here is that we all both lay, and clergy confess our sins to one another. If the clergy withheld their sinful deeds from the laity people begin to view them as pure, this is not so. All have sinned and fall short of the glory of God. Confession is a humbling experience which draws us all together, so we can see each other as human and in need of God's mercy and grace. Therefore, we are to confess to one another and pray for one another that we all might receive forgiveness for our sins.

Prayer: Father God in Heaven, we are told in your word to confess our sins with one another. Lord, send us a person with whom we feel confident to share our deep dark secrets. Even so Father God if there is not one who you will send we know we can come to you with our burdens and ask for forgiveness; removing the barrier between us and you. Father help us to not harm those who come to us with their unconfessed sins. Help us to be wise counsel and spiritually fit to comfort those brothers and sisters who share their unconfessed sin in our presence. Lord, this we ask in the name of the Father, Son and Holy Spirit. Amen

Day 268

remember this: Whoever turns a sinner from the error
of his way will save him from death and cover over a
multitude of sins. (James 5:20 NIV)

As you guide sinful people to Christ and they come bringing their
broken hearts to a merciful Savior, you are accomplishing a good work.
Once a person is converted to believing in Christ Jesus they are freed
from the condemnation of facing an eternal blazing hell with the devil
and his angels. Our loving God will blot out all sins committed when
that person comes to faith in Jesus.

Prayer: Lord God Almighty Our Merciful Father, we your hand made
servants need an infusion of grace to aid us in accepting correction
and giving correction to others as we all are stained by sin. Father
God as we see others living in sin help us to sensitively show them the
error of their ways as we seek to guide them back to the narrow path
which is illuminated by Jesus the light of the world. Help us and them
come to Jesus which leads to a right relationship with you. As others
confront us with our sins help us to receive that correction and be
restored likewise. This we pray in Jesus' name. Amen

Day 269

[23]Then He said to them all, "If anyone desires to come
after Me, let him deny himself, and take up his cross
daily, and follow Me.[24]For whoever desires to save his
life will lose it, but whoever loses his life for My sake
will save it. (Luke 9:23-24 NKJV)

There is a cost involved with following Jesus. It is first self-denial.
Denial of the flesh is perhaps one of the most difficult things for a
person to do. In todays' society, the church proclaims abstinence in
sexual situations for our children and they say it is impossible. The
church says to give in support of its ministry and people say I don't

have enough. God has said moderation in all things, people say I can't get enough. We have the obligation to bear up under the lusts of the flesh; rejecting feeding it. This is our cross to bear daily. When you think about it isn't it a light burden.

Prayer: Lord God Almighty our Master and Maker, we come to you in the name of Jesus asking that you forgive us for our self-centered lifestyles. We are constantly looking for shortcuts through life; including a means to salvation. Help us Lord to bear the burden of our cross daily and deny self and live for you; place our faith in Christ alone. Help us to live as we die to self. This we pray in Jesus' name. Amen

Day 270

Know this, my beloved brothers: let every person be quick to hear, slow to speak, slow to anger. (James 1:19 ESV)

When God in his infinite wisdom created mankind, he gave us two ears and one mouth. We should listen twice as much as we speak. Many people operate in just the opposite manner and speak more than listen. When we open our mouths offering dialogue without the benefit of thought we demonstrate ourselves to be ignorant and callous. When others do this to us we become angry, saying "how could they" be so inconsiderate. Let Jesus be your guide. When Jesus was wrongfully accused, he said not a word. Jesus says learn from him, he is gentle and humble of heart. Be quiet and listen. Speak only concerning subjects you are knowledgeable in. Do not become angry with someone for doing to you what you have done to others.

Prayer: Lord God Almighty hearer of prayers and hearts, we come in the name of Jesus thanking you for being there and listening when we present our prayers to you. Imprint on our hearts that we should become good listeners who hear others before speaking. Help us to show care and concern for one another by listening to each other and loving each other. This we pray in Jesus' name. Amen

Day 271

Do not let any unwholesome talk come out of your mouths, but only what is helpful for building others up according to their needs, that it may benefit those who listen. (Ephesians 4:29 NIV)

Objectionable language is often heard in the halls of schools, within the walls of homes and on the campuses of churches. When one human being wants to discredit another they often begin with condescending dialog about the person they are speaking out against. Politicians are known for using this tactic in campaign speechmaking. We only think we know other people; the truth is we cannot know them because we do not live in their skin or think their thoughts. Let us speak words which promote the welfare, status and self-worth of the individual we are speaking of.

Prayer: Lord God Almighty whose words promote life, we children of men often tear each other down with unwholesome talk. Father God empower us with a spirit of encouragement rather than a spirit of discouragement. Father we ask this in Jesus' name. Amen

Day 272

and call upon me in the day of trouble; I will deliver you, and you shall glorify me. (Psalm 50:15 ESV)

Acknowledge your dependence of the God of creation in His fullness and truth; He will come to your rescue in times of trouble. Praise offerings is the first step for the child of God in receipt of His help. Remember as you ask for His help that you have made a vow to Him in saying you love Him. Jesus has said "If you love me you will keep my Commandments".

Prayer: Lord God Almighty our Ever-Present Help in times of trouble, we think ourselves strong, but the only true strength Father God is found in you. Thank you, Lord God, that we can remain reliant on you in every situation of life. Thank you that you afford us an opportunity to call on you when trouble arises. Help us to be obedient to you in all things you have commanded. Thank you that in Christ Jesus we have the deliverer who will carry us to eternal life which will remove us from the trouble of life in this world. In Jesus' name, we pray. Amen

Day 273

Then he said to them, "Go your way. Eat the fat and drink sweet wine and send portions to anyone who has nothing ready, for this day is holy to our Lord. And do not be grieved, for the joy of the LORD is your strength." (Nehemiah 8:10 ESV)

On joyous occasions when large portions of food are prepared for family feasts do we remember the less fortunate? On holidays like, Christmas, Thanksgiving, Easter and New Years after the celebration is over do you have food to discard? That could have been given to the less fortunate, like the homeless who scrounge daily for sustenance. Let us be better stewards of God's bounty in our lives. Every day is an opportunity to see God's provision in your life.

Prayer: Lord God Almighty our Strength, forgive us for not walking in the power you give us. Help us to help others through leaning on you as our strength. Help us to understand that it is through our relationship with you that a great power and obligation has been bestowed upon us by you. Empower us to share the joy you have given us with those who lack joy. In Jesus' name, we pray. Amen

Day 274

Whoever gives heed to instruction prospers and blessed is he who trusts in the Lord. (Proverbs 16:20 NIV)

Only through living out the Word of God can we find our true path through this life. There is instruction in God's Word for those who take the time to read, study and meditate on it. Trust in the Lord and you cannot go wrong.

Prayer: Lord God Almighty who instructs his people, Father we thank you in the name of Jesus for instruction on how to dwell with one another on this earth. We thank you Father for the Bible: B-Basic, I-Instructions, B-Before, L-Leaving, E-Earth, which tells us about your love, how we should interact with one another and to watch out for the snares of this world and the lord of this world who would destroy us and our opportunity for eternal life. Father we thank you in the name of Jesus. Amen

Day 275

> You shall no more be termed Forsaken, and your land shall no more be termed Desolate, but you shall be called My Delight Is in Her, and your land Married; for the Lord delights in you, and your land shall be married. (Isaiah 62:4 ESV)

When God is in control your house becomes a place of prosperity not a place of desolation. Where God dwells, there is provision. Where God does not dwell, there is lack. God delights to give all good things to those who call on the name of Jesus.

Prayer: Lord God Almighty the God of Reconciliation, in the name of Jesus we thank you for no longer seeing us as forsaken but married to you through the church. Lord we are now in relationship with you through the marriage of the church where Christ is the bridegroom and the church is the bride. Thank you for such a loving relationship where you delight in us. In Jesus name, we pray. Amen

Day 276

> [1]Blessed is he who considers the poor; The LORD will deliver him in time of trouble. [2]The LORD will preserve

him and keep him alive, And he will be blessed on the earth; You will not deliver him to the will of his enemies. (Psalm 41:1-2 NKJV)

If you have the authority, power, resources to help the less fortunate it is an opportunity for you to receive Heavenly blessing. When you do for those who cannot do for themselves God sees as you become defender of the weak, resource challenged or outcast. In seeing you as the White Knight in defense of the defenseless God views and blesses your efforts.

Prayer: Lord God Almighty the God of countless Blessings, only you Lord, can give victory when all else looks like defeat. You O God defend the powerless and come to their aid in times of trouble. Thank you, Lord for continued blessings amid life's trials and tribulations. Help us to recognize you at work in our lives. For this Lord God, we lift our hands and voices in praise to you; to you alone, belong all praise honor and glory forever and ever. In Jesus' name, we pray. Amen

Day 277

give thanks in all circumstances; for this is the will of God in Christ Jesus for you. (1 Thessalonians 5:18 ESV)

Gratitude is vital in our world. When someone does good toward you it is critical that you acknowledge their kindness in your life. Jesus gave thanks for those God the Father had given him, although they were broken, lacking in understanding, failing in total commitment and fearful. You and I ought to give thanks in all situations regardless of how dim the circumstances seem. God is there and in control of the final, outcome. Give thanks not because of the difficulties but as you proceed through them because God is ever present in your life.

Prayer: Heavenly Father God, we children of men find ourselves engulfed in varied situations as we pass through this thing called life. Father your word says to give thanks in all circumstances not for all circumstances. Lord God we may not be thankful for the loss of a loved one, but we can be thankful that you have received our loved one into that prepared place that awaits all who have placed their faith in Christ Jesus our Lord. We thank you for that place which you have prepared for your prepared people. Thank you that no matter how dark a situation may seem we can give thanks that you are in control of the outcome. In Jesus' name, we pray. Amen

Day 278

Jesus looked at them and said, "With man it is impossible, but not with God. For all things are possible with God." (Mark 10:27 ESV)

Faith in the finished work of the cross is sometimes wishy-washy at its best. People say they believe that an eternal life await them yet if they are threatened with the prospect of death they panic, begin crying, trembling and are fearful of that event overtaking them. This is because of a lack in unyielding belief that salvation and a better existence awaits. The truth is people think of this life and its obtained and unobtained wealth and events, wanting to hold onto it. Even the person whose body is wracked with pain desires to live rather than go home to be with Jesus. In our own power, we cannot face death but with God it is possible. Seek God's strength because death is inevitable.

Prayer: Most gracious Heavenly Father God, we are a people of Swiss cheese faith. Father we want to have faith which is solid as a rock please strengthen us. Help us Lord to see you at work in our lives and thereby increase our faith and subdue our unbelief. Lord we want to believe but with man this is impossible but with you God we know all things are possible. Lord do for us what we cannot do for ourselves. This we ask in Jesus' name. Amen

Day 279

In this meaningless life of mine I have seen both of these: a righteous man perishing in his righteousness, and a wicked man living long in his wickedness. (Ecclesiastes 7:15 NIV)

How is it that a person who seems to do good in the sight of others; living a wholesome life has multitudes of troubles befall them? Then that righteous person dies at what seems to us an early death. How is it that a person who cares little for humanity, who speaks lies, insults and cheat others, and exudes vulgar speech from their lips prosper and flourish? Then this person lives to a ripe old age. Righteous living does not guarantee protection against an early demise. The world expects just the opposite. God may allow these things to happen in his creation so just remember, "God's ways are not our ways" and we do not always know his purposes behind his "allowed" activities on this earth.

Prayer: O Lord our God, who on earth can know your ways? We know this one thing that in all things you are a righteous, loving and caring God. Lord we see the righteous perishing and the wicked flourishing, and we say, why? Help us to leave to you the conclusion of all things, and in our weak carnal minds not to judge how you the creator of all things should handle this world. Father you are God alone all by yourself and we yield to your discretion. Hear us we pray in Jesus' name. Amen

Day 280

Then I considered all that my hands had done and the toil I had expended in doing it, and behold, all was vanity and a striving after wind, and there was nothing to be gained under the sun. (Ecclesiastes 2:11 ESV)

As we begin to grow from childhood into adulthood we have ambitions which seem to be the most important thing in the world. After living for a few adult years, we come to learn that no matter how much we accomplish it does not completely satisfy. After all the striving, there is little to no satisfaction. Only what we do for the Lord gives fulfillment of the soul.

Prayer: O Lord our God Creator of all that was, is and ever shall be we all seek after those things this world has to offer which tells the rest of the world we have arrived. Help us to understand that true riches are those which are in the heavenly realm. Help us to use the riches of this world to help the less fortunate and under resourced. This we pray in Jesus' name. Amen

Day 281

> [3]When I consider your heavens, the work of your fingers, the moon and the stars, which you have set in place, [4]what is man that you are mindful of him, the son of man that you care for him? (Psalm 8:3-4 NIV)

The universe is full of great wonders. Look at the sun, moon and stars knowing that an omnipotent God created that. Look at the oceans, rivers, hills and mountains knowing that in His infinite wisdom God carved them out of the landscape of the earth. How small and insignificant is man in comparison to all of God's great creation, yet to Him we are more important than it all.

Prayer: Heavenly Father God, we see all you have done in the heavens and on the earth. We see the waters of the oceans whose boundaries you have established. We look to the heavens and see the vastness of it and how you have set in motion the rotation of the planets, galaxies and the universe. What an awesome God you are there is none like you; you are God all alone. With all your holiness, supremacy and power you are still mindful of us sinful human creatures. Thank you for never turning your face away from us. This we pray with gratitude in Jesus' name. Amen

Day 282

> The Spirit himself bears witness with our spirit that we are children of God. (Romans 8:16 NKJV)

Just as we understand our biological parent's presence in our lives and accept the fact that we are born of their bodies. The Holy Spirit of God authenticates to our spirit the truth that God is our Father and creator. That endorsement come when you get that warm internal sensation of security in knowing that your loving Father God watches your coming and going day in and day out.

Prayer: Lord God Almighty our Father, we thank you for the inner testimony of the Holy Spirit which reassures us if the relationship we have with you. We thank you that even sinners like us you call your children. Help us to live for you as an out pouring of the love we have for you and for each other. Father God order our steps, order our thoughts, order our words as we are guided by your Word. In Jesus' name, we pray. Amen

Day 283

> Then he said to them, "Watch out! Be on your guard
> against all kinds of greed; a man's life does not consist
> in the abundance of his possessions." (Luke 12:15 NIV)

Beware of avarice. In the game of life people are playing to obtain all the marbles. It is said, he who has the most toys at the end is the winner of the game. At the end is the key statement here. We all came into this world naked and bankrupt. We will all leave this world naked and penniless, since whatever you acquire in this life will be left behind for others. The important marbles to obtain is how have you improved the lives of those who you have met while alive. Cars, clothes, houses and diamond rings are not what is significant. Legacy of character is what lives on.

Prayer: Lord God Almighty our Provider, give us enough so that we are without want. As we seek our provision of daily bread give us a spirit of contentment so that we do not dishonor the supply you provide, for the earth and the fullness thereof belongs to you. Empower us to be

Godly and content with that which comes from your hand. This we ask in Jesus' name. Amen

Day 284

So, if the Son sets you free, you will be free indeed. (John 8:36 NIV)

Jesus has come and removed the encumbrance of works righteousness. We children of men find it difficult to face the fact that salvation is free. We feel we must do something to earn salvation; the world we live in has taught us from birth nothing is free. True, in this world we must earn everything we desire even love from another human being. There is however one thing we can be certain of, that Jesus came and offers the "free gift" of grace which leads to salvation as we place our faith in him. Through Jesus we are free from seeking to earn salvation. Jesus freely offers it to any who would receive it.

Prayer: Lord God in Heaven Our Father, we often carry the baggage of past sin with us into our present. The adversary seeks to make us believe that our sin was so grievous that you O God cannot and will not forgive us. Help all to understand that this is a trick of the enemy which perpetuates the lie that we are not forgiven by the shedding of the blood of the Lamb, Jesus Christ your Son our Savior. Thank you Father God the through Christ Jesus your son we are reconciled to you and now free indeed. In Jesus' name, we pray. Amen

Day 285

And we, who with unveiled faces all reflect the Lord's glory, are being transformed into his likeness with ever-increasing glory, which comes from the Lord, who is the Spirit. (2 Corinthians 3:18 NIV)

Christ's glory is his divine quality. Christ demonstrated His divinity by carrying our sins to the cross of Calvary. Even more important is the fact that He rose three days later demonstrating that we who place our faith in Him shall one day also rise to eternal glory with Him. As we learn more about our savior we come to know Him as God. As we draw near to Him through the study of His word we are being transformed into His likeness. Being transformed we begin to live according to His word and live in harmony with each other which is divinely granted to us through the Holy Spirit.

Prayer: Lord God Almighty, we are just everyday people. Father God we seek to be more like Jesus each day of our life walk. Lord we cannot accomplish this on our own but only through the power of your Holy Spirit. Help us to work the works of Christ as we seek to grow and be like him in every way. Transform us O God. This we ask in Jesus' name. Amen

Day 286

> But he said to her, "You speak as one of the foolish women would speak. Shall we receive good from God, and shall we not receive evil?" In all this Job did not sin with his lips. (Job 2:10 ESV)

We see the goodness and multiple blessing the Lord God has bestowed upon us or our loved ones. But let trouble come and some people think that God has abandoned them. Job's wife felt that way and told Job to curse God and die. God gives us all good things, but he does not give us bad things. Even in the case of Job God allowed the catastrophe, God did not cause it. Sometimes there are testing times in the life of even the most resolute Christian. It is those trying time that are troubling times when we must rely on the strength of the Lord to sustain us. Lean on Jesus for comfort when trouble comes. Remember he is our High Priest who was tempted just as we are being tempted.

Prayer: O LORD our God and Father, we have good times and we have necessary times which bring us to our knees. It is in the trying and troubling times that we seek you out with the determination of a drowning man. Thank you, Father God for the good you bring into our lives and thank you for allowing us to experience the difficulties which shape and mold us into the image of Christ as we learn to lean not to our own understanding but to lean on you. Thank you for all that comes from you. LORD, hear our prayer in Jesus' name. Amen

Day 287

> But I say, walk by the Spirit, and you will not gratify the
> desires of the flesh. (Galatians 5:16 ESV)

The flesh is sinful by nature. Our human nature is corrupt because of inherited sin passed down from Adam. The flesh wants to be fed whatever it desires, whether that is mind and mood-altering substances, food, sex, wealth or power. The works of the flesh dominate the weak whose faith is supported on gossamer knowledge of who and what God is. Seek the Holy Spirit who makes you holy by bringing you to faith in Christ Jesus. In doing this you can learn through the Spirit to live a Godly life based on Heavenly values which lead to life rather than earthly values which lead to eternal death.

Prayer: Father God in Heaven, we are often under the influence of something in this life. Many are found to be under the influence of money, alcohol, drugs, sex, tobacco, sports, music and many other things which we allow to influence our actions and lives. Help us poor sinful beings, O God to be only under the influence of your Holy Spirit. Help us to yield to the Spirit of life that we might be filled and directed by his power alone. Lord, hear our prayer in Jesus' name. Amen

Day 288

> But when he saw the wind boisterous, he was afraid;
> and beginning to sink, he cried, saying, Lord, save me.
> (Matthew 14:30 NKJV)

Are you sinking in a sea of bad decisions, ethical decay and distress associated with these? Cry out to Jesus saying, "Lord save me". He can, and he will, if you just call him. Peter walked on what others would sink in. This accomplishment was achieved when Peter kept his focus on Christ. When you place your focus on what is in your surroundings rather than Christ, the miracle of divine provision comes to an end.

Prayer: Lord Jesus, we children of men all experience being tossed and driven by the rough seas of life. Lord in the middle of our constant struggle against the buffeting you are ever walking towards us. There are some Lord who seek to join you by walking on what others sink in and there are those who are too afraid to step out of the boat constructed by worldly values, thinking it safer there. Lord, give us boldness to walk on the rough waters of life. Lord, give us confidence in you which helps us to get out of the boat and come to you regardless of all the tumult that is occurring around us. Lord in your Mercy hear our prayer. Amen

Day 289

Now faith is the substance of things hoped for, the evidence of things not seen. (Hebrews 11:1 NKJV)

If you want something and decide the best possible way to get it is to work harder for it, that is faith in action. As you work and save, the vision of your objective becomes clearer and clearer. In your mind's eye, you see the desire of your heart in vivid detail until the day arrives and you can then take the deposited money and exchange it for your tangible object. If you are in Christ Jesus, your hope is rooted in a future life in the Heavenly Kingdom Jesus has prepared for you. So, continue to hold onto the faith being cultivated by the Holy Spirit which is making deposits in your heart. The time is coming when the unseen will one day become the seen. In your spiritual eyes, you must see it in the spiritual before you see it in the natural.

Prayer: Lord, help us to place our faith in you alone. Help us to know that despite the circumstances we find ourselves in, you can deliver us as your will permits. In Christ Jesus, we pray. Amen

Day 290

> And it shall come to pass that everyone who calls on
> the name of the Lord shall be saved. For in Mount Zion
> and in Jerusalem there shall be those who escape, as
> the Lord has said, and among the survivors shall be
> those whom the Lord calls. (Joel 2:32 ESV)

To call on the name of the Lord is to worship Him and to pray to Him in the full knowledge that He is Creator of all things and He is Sovereign. God has come to earth in the form of human kind, to save us from condemnation by the adversary who accuses us as he himself tempts us to sinful activity. God through Christ has called us out of the darkness of sin into the wonderful light of His salvation.

Prayer: Lord God Almighty, who can we call on in our life struggle but you? We call on you O merciful IAM as the only path to eternal life. Father as you hear us call you through Christ Jesus you say welcome, "come and share your master's happiness". This we pray in the name of Jesus. Amen

Day 291

> If you do well, will you not be accepted? And if you do
> not do well, sin is crouching at the door. Its desire is for
> you, but you must rule over it." (Genesis 4:7 ESV)

The old is past and we are now in the new, this happens each twenty-four-hour cycle which we call a day. This is the time for new beginnings. Unfortunately, we could not leave the blemish of sin in the past it continually follows us seeking to influence our actions. Seek diligently to be righteous in all things as much as is within you. Seek the Lord before you attempt your daily activities asking for his protection, guidance and the power of his word to help you fend off the devil and his encouragements. You must fight the sin that seeks to overtake you

Prayer: Heavenly Father our Lord and our God, we are constantly pursued by sin. Lord by the power of your Holy Spirit, be the sentry at the doors to our hearts so that sin may not enter in and seduce us to walk out of fellowship with you. Lord, guard us against pride, anger, lust, greed, murder and envy. Master, this we ask in Jesus' name. Amen

Day 292

A double minded man is unstable in all his ways. (James 1:8 KJV)

The old adage you can't play both sides of the fence holds true. The way to look at playing both sides of the fence is the person is a hypocrite who say one thing to one person and something entirely different to another. This is instability and there is no integrity in a person who does such things. If a person will not take a position and stand by it on one viewpoint, do not expect him to be faithful to any perspective. Jesus taught of the rich young man who chose his riches rather than following the Kingdom of God. He at least chose a position.

Prayer: Gracious God our Father, we children of men come to you asking your guidance and inspiration then when you reveal the answer we rethink what you have shared with us. Lord this often happens when our will does not align with your will and we allow our self-will to run riot over our affairs. Lord God Heavenly Father forgive us for being double minded. Father God in the name of Jesus help us to benefit from past mistakes as you graciously correct and redirect our lives and our actions. This we pray in Jesus' name. Amen

Day 293

Those whom I love I rebuke and discipline. So be
earnest, and repent. (Revelation 3:19 NIV)

If you are a parent or guardian of a child, you know that a time of
disciplining a child is one of seeking correct action from the child.
This is true of our Heavenly Father as well. God our Father censures us
through his word and then there are times of scolding as the word of God
convicts us when we know better yet do not do better. God's discipline
guides us to repentance so that we might grow in our Christian walk.
Scolding, discipline and correction does not mean God does not love
us, quite the opposite is true. Those whom God loves he tells them
their sinful faults, because sin breaks the relationship between God
and mankind. This is done by the Father so that they can repent and
become better as the relationship is strengthened and reinstated. The
Blood of Jesus washes us clean as repentance removes sin.

Prayer: Father God, no discipline is comfortable, yet your discipline
Father God creates change that is necessary. Father your discipline
refines like the fire purifies silver and gold. Lord God almighty, give
us a repentant heart that we may be found favorable in your sight. In
Jesus' name, we pray. Amen

Day 294

But in your hearts set apart Christ as Lord. Always be
prepared to give an answer to everyone who asks you
to give the reason for the hope that you have. But do
this with gentleness and respect. (1 Peter 3:15 NIV)

If as a Christian, you have ever entered a conversation with a person of
another denomination or religion you may have experienced it quickly
escalating into a heated discussion. Because you love the Lord and
know Him as the savior of the world you want others to share in your
great fortune. The truth is everyone will not be saved. Your duty is to

share that Jesus loves them and cares for them and He alone is their salvation. Jesus shed His blood for the believer and those who right now do not believe but may one day believe if not too late. You plant the seed then let the Holy Spirit do His work in changing hardened hearts. Share the Gospel with kindness and revere God's name by doing so peacefully.

Prayer: Holy and Loving Father God, thank you for the grace found in Christ Jesus. We like others may not have heard your message of salvation coming from any other source other than another human being. Give us the conviction needed to share the hope offered through Jesus in a way that reflects your grace. Through Christ Jesus the Living Hope we pray. Amen

Day 295

> But the Lord said to Samuel, "Do not look on his appearance or on the height of his stature, because I have rejected him. For the Lord sees not as man sees: man looks on the outward appearance, but the Lord looks on the heart." (1 Samuel 16:7 ESV)

We children of men look at the aesthetically pleasing which is often our determining factor for offering our support, love and alliance to an individual. Samuel was doing the same thing when God sent him to anoint the future king of Israel. Our standards are the same as those of the LORD God Almighty. God knows the heart of every person as well as their end before their beginning.

Prayer: O Lord our God, in you alone there is no reproach. Father God you see beyond the carnal, viewing with spiritual discernment which views that which is unseen to the human eye. Lord God our Father instill in us just a fraction of that spiritual discernment as we observe each other. Lord we look at the exterior but you O God look at the heart. Help us to discern the inner disposition rather than the outer appearance. This we ask in Jesus' name. Amen

Day 296

And whatever you do, in word or deed, do everything
in the name of the Lord Jesus, giving thanks to God the
Father through him. (Colossians 3:17 ESV)

It is inconceivable that a criminal would begin his caper by going down
on his knees asking God for a successful wrongdoing. God created us
to do good works, not to do corrupt works. All our works should begin
by asking the guidance of our perfect God so that our works might be
crowned with success. Doing everything in the name of the Lord Jesus
invites our efforts to act rationally and with reverent intent.

Prayer: Lord God Heavenly Father, we approach you in the name of
Jesus asking your forgiveness for sins past, both known and unknown.
Help us to place you first in all that we say, think and do. Help us to
do all the works of our hands in the name of Jesus that you Lord God
through Christ Jesus may receive the honor and glory. This we pray in
Jesus' name. Amen

Day 297

[6]Do not eat the food of a stingy man, do not crave his
delicacies; [7]for he is the kind of man who is always
thinking about the cost. "Eat and drink," he says to
you, but his heart is not with you. (Proverbs 23:6-7 NIV)

Some people say one thing but mean something entirely different. A
stingy person is double minded, two faced and really does not want to
give out of generosity. The stingy give with hypocrisy. They give with a
heart thinking do not accept what is being laid out before you because
I don't want you to have it. When the stingy offer it is out of pretense.

Prayer: O Lord God our Redeemer, regard the hearts of your people and
remove that which is unacceptable. Lord, out of the mouth comes the
abundance of the heart and as a person thinks so is he in his heart.

Help us O God for there is no other help we know. This we pray in Jesus' name. Amen

Day 298

Anyone who does not love does not know God, because God is love. (1 John 4:8 ESV)

Only through having an intimate relationship with God can a person truly know and express love. God's precious love is demonstrated in the body of the incarnate Jesus Christ. Jesus came to earth as an atoning sacrifice for every person ever born or who will ever be born until Jesus' return to earth on "The day of the Lord". To love like Jesus is to love in a sacrificial manner. If you find no love in a person that person has no relationship with the Lord God Almighty.

Prayer: Lord God our Father in Heaven, you loved us before we came into this place; by the name of Jesus you in your love will carry us away from this place. Thank you, LORD, for the unconditional love you offer. Help us to love unconditionally. Father God, mankind loves because of, you Lord God loves "In Spite Of". Hear our prayer in Jesus' name. Amen

Day 299

That if you confess with your mouth, "Jesus is Lord," and believe in your heart that God raised him from the dead, you will be saved. (Romans 10:9 NIV)

Salvation is as easy as A, B, C. Accept Jesus Christ as your Lord and Savior, **believe** that God raised Jesus from the dead and Confess that with your mouth then salvation is yours. Jesus died for us all on a hill called Calvary that we might be offered salvation through his sacrificial act. All mankind need do is receive and believe that Jesus died for them and they will be saved.

Prayer: Lord God Almighty, we children of men have opportunities of witnessing for Christ Jesus presented to us daily. Prayerfully we ask you to imbed in us a spirit of testimony that we can share the good news of Christ's love for us and his selfless act at Calvary to win salvation for all mankind. Father God hear our prayer in Jesus' name. Amen

Day 300

For we are his workmanship, created in Christ Jesus for
good works, which God prepared beforehand, that we
should walk in them. (Ephesians 2:10 NKJV)

Isn't it amazing that God in his infinite wisdom knew us before we were born on this earth? Any worthwhile deed you perform was pre-ordained by God so that someone would benefit from it. In some case's you are the benefactor and in other cases you are the recipient. When we align ourselves with Christ and his love, we then can express our love for one another through acts of kindness.

Prayer: Abba God, we your hand made servants were created to do good works for the benefit of mankind. Father God you did this through Christ Jesus before the foundation of the world was completed. Thank you for adding us in your plan. Help us to carry out the work you intend for us to accomplish through the help of the Holy Spirit. This we pray in Jesus' name. Amen

Day 301

but God shows his love for us in that while we were still
sinners, Christ died for us. (Romans 5:8 ESV)

We live in a world where numbers are used to determine success or failure. People are graphed, charted, marginalized or elevated using numbers to plot human perception of life status. Through numbers people think the larger organization is the better organization, the smaller is the lesser. Fortunately for mankind our Lord and Savior Jesus Christ does not operate in like manner. Jesus died for us individually as we faithfully accept his death for our benefit. We all are sinners and Jesus died for the sins of each of us. And because of his death we each one by one will be welcomed into his kingdom, there to live with him through all eternity. The most important number is one, one God, one Lord, one savior, one Christ Jesus and one you.

Prayer: Lord God of Salvation, your love is beyond our feeble comprehension. Father God you allowed Christ to die for us while we continued in our sinful state. Thank you, Lord. Our hearts are filled with gratitude. Thank you. In Jesus' name, we pray. Amen

Day 302

Let us hear the conclusion of the whole matter: Fear
God and keep his commandments: for this is the whole
duty of man. (Ecclesiastes 12:13 KJV)

After following the crowd, supposedly lifting yourself by your own boot straps or being a self-made person, the question is, have you been fulfilled. As one of God's creatures we have an obligation to fulfill. In fulfilling God's purpose for your life, you find fulfillment. The Bible teaches us to revere and honor God by keeping his directives, laws and instructions. In doing so we are in alignment with what God has intended for us as his hand made servants. Whatever his commands they are for our good because God will never harm us.

Prayer: Almighty and Everlasting Lord our God, we children of men get into trouble when we attempt to outguess you and your actions. Father we attempt to operate in self-will rather than God will. LORD in your mercy help us to live out to the best of our ability your commandments and to have a respectful awe of who you are. Father this is the duty of mankind, help us to live it until Christ returns for us. In Jesus name, we pray. Amen

Day 303

Now we have received not the spirit of the world, but the
Spirit who is from God, that we might understand the
things freely given us by God. (1 Corinthians 2:12 NKJV)

The wisdom of this age tells us, if it feels good touch it, if it tastes
good eat it, if it looks good watch it. In other words, the spirit of this
world is sensual, filled with avarice, lust, gluttony and perversion and
self-interest. The spirit of the world ends in death. When you submit
to the spirit of the world you alienate yourself from God's Holy Spirit
which leads to life. God through Christ Jesus has conveyed upon those
whose faith is in Jesus the Holy Spirit. The Spirit of God teaches us the
things of God that we may live Godly lives as we await the return of
our redeemer Jesus Christ.

Prayer: Lord God our ever-giving Father, there are many spirits in
this world who would like to unite with your children. Father God the
world did not give us a spirit of life, but you did. Lord the spirits of the
world cause strife and turmoil, but your Spirit brings concord. Lord,
purge from us the spirits of the world and infuse us with your Holy
Spirit alone. Help us Lord through the power of your Holy Spirit to
understand the things you have freely given us through Christ Jesus.
In Jesus' name, we pray. Amen

Day 304

Jesus said to him, "I am the way, and the truth, and the
life. No one comes to the Father except through me.
(John 14:6 NKJV)

You may have heard people say that all religion leads to the same God;
because God is the same, all people can get to the afterlife reward he
has for us. Unfortunately for those who are Muslim, Jewish or some
other world religion and afterlife with the God who created all things
this is impossible. Only in the Christian faith where the Triune God

is served can there be an expectation to live with God in eternity. The same God who created all things came to earth as a human being named Jesus. Jesus died for the sins of mankind carrying those sins to the grave. Three days later Jesus rose from death to demonstrate that those who believed in him as savior of the world, could expect to rise also from death to eternal life. After Jesus left earth he sent his Holy Spirit to teach us and guide us through life. Jesus is the only way into eternity.

Prayer: Lord Jesus I invite you into my life. I ask you Lord to order my steps, direct my speech, make my thoughts obedient to your will and purify my touch. Lord I submit wholly to your Holy will. Lord I acknowledge you as my Lord and Savior. Lord please accept me into your kingdom when my final day of life here on earth come. Lord we pray this in the name of the Father, Son and Holy Spirit. Amen

Day 305

> But to all who did receive him, who believed in his name, he gave the right to become children of God. (John 1:12 ESV)

When Jesus came to earth a universal invitation was issued to all mankind to accept Jesus the Messiah who would bring all people back into a right relationship with the creator Father God. Still today many rejects that offer. No matter how vile the sinner they can claim God's mercy through the atoning sacrifice of Jesus. That sacrifice of his precious blood gave anyone who accepted him the right to heirship as a child of the Living God. What an honor it is to be called a "child of God".

Prayer: Lord God Heavenly Father, thank you for your faithful grace. Thank you, Lord God for welcoming us into your family through Christ Jesus. Hear us as we confess our belief in his name for salvation and eternal life. Father God, we await the day when we will be with you in eternity. In Jesus' name, we pray. Amen

Day 306

But you have been anointed by the Holy One, and you
all have knowledge. (1 John 2:20 NRSV)

God's Holy Spirit has come upon all mankind shedding the truth of
God and how he cares for his people. The anointing of the Holy Spirit
teaches us what we need to know for our salvation. What we need to
know is that Jesus the Christ died for our sins; because of his death
and resurrection we are offered eternal life. Only those on whom and
in whom the Holy Spirit rests know this. Those who have rejected the
person and power of the Holy Spirit are without this knowledge.

Prayer: Holy and Eternal Lord God Almighty, we children of men often
act with carnal behavior which is not within your will. Forgive us for
forgetting the anointing you have placed on us Holy One. Bring to the
forefront of our minds all the divine knowledge you have shared with us
through your Word. Lord God forgive us where we fall short. Quicken us
to be the people you desire us to be. This we ask in Jesus' name. Amen

Day 307

What then shall we say to these things? If God is for us,
who can be against us? (Romans 8:31 ESV)

Living in a world full of strife and turmoil it is a comfort to know that
an omnipotent, omnipresent, omniscient God is watching out for our
wellbeing. Because God is love and he demonstrate his love towards
us daily, we can be assured of his purpose towards us. When you
are overshadowed by God's grace, mercy and favor, who can stand
against you?

Prayer: Lord God Heavenly Father, you watch over your people day and
night. Lord, you neither slumber nor sleep and your vigilance protects
us from hurt, harm and danger. Father you know our ending before
our beginning. What an awesome and mighty God you are and yet you

care so much for us. Thank you, LORD, for your constant protection of those who you have called and justified through Christ Jesus. In Jesus' Holy name we pray. Amen

Day 308

> Let me hear in the morning of your steadfast love, for
> in you I trust. Make me know the way I should go, for
> to you I lift up my soul. (Psalm 143:8 ESV)

As we awaken to face a new day we may ask God to speak words of encouragement into our otherwise obstacle strewn lives. We should pray that our first conscious thoughts be directed by the orchestrater of the universe. We can find no better instructor for our beginning. Place your confidence in no other.

Prayer: O Lord our God who created the Heavens and the Earth, speak to us as we awaken each day. O God be not silent as we begin our daily trek through life. Lord God guide us, direct us; O God show us which path to follow as we lift our souls to you. Help us to travel the corridor you lay before us. This we ask in Jesus' name. Amen

Day 309

> And going a little farther he fell on his face and prayed,
> saying, "My Father, if it be possible, let this cup pass
> from me; nevertheless, not as I will, but as you will."
> (Matthew 26:39 ESV)

We find Jesus in the garden of Gethsemane, knowing the suffering and pain his flesh was about to go through, ask to be spared this suffering. But, we also see Jesus saying, Father your will be done. If mankind would allow God's Holy will to be done on this earth, we would have a world of peace. The problem is that everyone has a will of their own which they want enacted. When one person's will collide with the will of another person tensions rise and conflict ensues. Let us follow Christ who was about to suffer unthinkable torture and death following God's divine will rather than the will of his flesh.

Prayer: Heavenly Father our God of compassion, many are the times when we children of men must suffer the adversities of this life. Yet, Father God as we are occupied with the struggle we can remember Christ Jesus who also experienced the same struggles as we. Thank you, Father God, that Christ endured the ultimate struggle of death for our sakes. Father as we continue in life's struggle help us to speak the words "nevertheless not my will but your will be done". In Jesus' name we pray. Amen

Day 310

> I will sing to the Lord, for he has been good to me.
> (Psalms 13:6 NIV)

I live in a community outside away from the hustle and bustle of the city. When I awaken in the morning and go out to retrieve the paper or for whatever reason, I hear the birds singing in the trees. I like the think that even God's lesser creatures sing songs of praise to him for a new day.

Prayer: Lord God Almighty, we cannot begin to express all the goodness you have done throughout our lives. Father your greatest acts of goodness are your coming as the incarnate God to dwell among your people and ultimately die on the cross of Calvary that they might receive the freely offered gift of salvation. In the name of Jesus, we lift our voices in gratitude. Amen

Day 311

> To do what is right and just is more acceptable to the
> Lord than sacrifice. (Proverbs 21:3 NIV)

When your heart is not right your sacrifices to God receive no veneration from him. This is what happened to Cain. It happens today to those who are poor stewards of God's bountiful gifts. These gifts include body, mind, financial resources, talents and worship. God detests wickedness in any form. Abusing your body with mind and mood-altering substances is not doing right. Not giving to God what is already his in the form of offerings for the work in his kingdom building purposes. Not using your God given talents to glorify him through your productivity. Giving God halfhearted worship by putting on your church face on Sunday and living for the world the rest of the week leads no one to Christ. The Lord prefers that you live according to his words given to his disciples. Love the Lord your God with all your heart and with all your soul and with all your mind and with all your strength. 'Love your neighbor as yourself.' This is right and just.

Prayer: Father God in Heaven, we approach you in the name of Jesus with a broken and contrite heart. Lord forgive us for not always doing what is right and just. We spend a few hours in worship on Sundays and some even practice fasting as a sacrifice to you. Teach our souls Lord to know that doing what is just and right is more acceptable to you than sacrifice. Lord Jesus, help us. We pray this in the name of the Father Son and Holy Spirit. Amen

Day 312

and raised us up with him and seated us with him in
the heavenly places in Christ Jesus. (Ephesians 2:6 ESV)

Jesus Christ died to atone for the sins of the world. He laid in a grave for three days but on the third day rose in glorious victory over Satan and death. Because of Jesus' shed blood we are vindicated in the eyes of God the Father. We now through this selfless act of our savior have a seat awaiting us in the Heavenly place where God resides.

Prayer: Lord God our Heavenly Father, you have raised us up and connected us to one another through Christ Jesus. Help us to love, support each other and walk in unity while we are yet on this side of the cross. Give us the wisdom to repair the ethnic, economic and

creedal divisions which exist between us. LORD, this we pray in Jesus'
name. Amen

Day 313

> So, then every one of us shall give account of himself
> to God. (Romans 14:12 KJV)

There is a final day of judgment coming when all men both living, and
dead will stand before the judgment throne of Christ. There we will give
answer for what was said and done throughout our lives. Therefore,
be encouraged to develop your faith relationship with Christ Jesus
who will pronounce you as one of his redeemed even in the face of the
shortcomings of this life that you initiated and participated in. Jesus
wishes that none be lost. Place your faith in him alone

Prayer: Our Father in Heaven, the day is surely coming when we all will
stand before you to give an account of our every action. All, Father God
will come with heads hung low. But many will hang their heads lower
than others. Thank you, Father God, that we will all be able to lift our
heads because of the redemption given us through Christ Jesus as he
says this one is mine. In Jesus' name, we pray. Amen

Day 314

> But if not, be it known to you, O king, that we will not
> serve your gods or worship the golden image that you
> have set up. (Daniel 3:18 NKJV)

Like the three Hebrews boys who challenged a king and death for
their belief that they serve a God who has the power to defy death. We
should stand steadfast and assured that God is standing in defense of
our wellbeing regardless of what the situation looks like. Our mindset
should be even if he does not save us from destruction he has the power
to do so. If he allows our demise it is for his purpose that this has
occurred. Serve God alone, no other entity can save you.

Prayer: O Lord our God the Great IAM, forgive us for placing so much value on things other than you. We place high value on our homes, cars, cash, companions and vocations. Help us O God to serve you and you alone. This we pray in Jesus' name. Amen

Day 315

The Lord has taken away the judgments against you; he has cleared away your enemies. The King of Israel, the Lord, is in your midst; you shall never again fear evil. (Zephaniah 3:15 ESV)

One punishment we all must endure and taste, is the sting of death, which was brought by the enemy of mankind. For those who place their faith in Jesus Christ as Lord and Savior. For those knowing God the Father offered Jesus up to die for our sins and then raised him from the dead so that we too may be raised on the last day. For all who embrace Jesus, the enemy and his death will not come a second time. For those who do not receive Jesus as Lord and Savior the enemy of death will come a second time casting them into the eternal darkness away from the presence of God. Our redeeming Savior has defeated Satan and death so that you will not be cast out of the presence of God but will live eternally with him in the New Jerusalem.

Prayer: O Lord our God and King, do remember us as we continue our earthly walk. Lord God Almighty you are never afar off. Calm and remove the calamity of our fearful lack of total trust in you. Lord, reassure us you are in our midst with the peace that only comes through you. In Jesus' name, we pray. Amen

Day 316

Set a guard over my mouth, O Lord; keep watch over the door of my lips. (Psalm 141:3 NIV)

There are times in our lives when we open our mouths and out pours words that we do not want spoken. Once a word is spoken it cannot be taken back it has revealed what is in your heart. Out of the mouth the heart speaks. We should always ask the Spirit of God to stand as a sentinel over our speech that no unwholesome talk may proceed from our lips.

Prayer: Lord God Almighty, when you created man you gave him two ears and one mouth. It has been said that this indicates we should listen twice as much as we talk. Father perhaps another way of looking at this is that with one mouth we do not have the dual capacity to speak evil against one another. Lord, with two ears we have the capacity to hear twice as much good about another. Lord God keep us from speaking evil into and about the lives of one another. Lord God our Creator hear our prayer in Jesus' name. Amen

Day 317

> Rather, speaking the truth in love, we are to grow up
> in every way into him who is the head, into Christ.
> (Ephesians 4:15 ESV)

It is difficult to speak the truth to people when you know that truth will hurt. However, when you speak the truth in love, God will enable the words of your mouth to be received as a healing ointment rather than an abrasive irritant. Jesus spoke to people in truth even if the recipient was uncomfortable with the statements. Follow Christ's example and be a deliverer of truth as he was.

Prayer: Our Father who is in Heaven, your word says the truth shall set you free. Help us Lord to speak the truth even when to do so may be painful for us or others. Give us the ability to speak in love and grow in the grace of Christ who is the head of our lives. In Jesus' name, we pray. Amen

Day 318

Your kingdom come, your will be done, on earth as it
is in heaven. (Matthew 6:10 NIV)

As we pray the prayer Jesus taught his disciples we come to this portion
which says, "your kingdom come, your will be done". Asking this is
asking that Jesus returns and claim his own or that this earth be over
shadowed with the same peace, love and harmony that will be found
in the Heavenly kingdom when Jesus returns. Jesus' will be that we all
will one day live with him in his prepared place that he has prepared
for his prepared people.

Prayer: Lord God Almighty, if we could have anything Lord give us
your kingdom on earth. Lord we live in a world where people are
cruel towards one another. Lord, people are backbiting, clawing and
clamoring for position so they are above and beyond the rest. Father
God you are love. Bloom love in the hearts of all people so that we
live by kingdom principles and there be peace on earth and goodwill
towards each other. Lord let your kingdom come. In Jesus name, we
pray this. Amen

Day 319

So, do not fear, for I am with you; do not be dismayed,
for I am your God. I will strengthen you and help
you; I will uphold you with my righteous right hand.
(Isaiah 41:10 NIV)

Fear strikes in the hearts of mankind because we fear both failure
as well as success. We fear the known and the unknown. Some fears
are self-generated and hold no validity. Other fears are needed for
self-preservation. God seeks to calm our fears by assuring us that he
is always with us. Remember fear is the absence of faith. He has said
never will I leave you or forsake you. When fear strikes ask God for his
assured presence.

Prayer: Heavenly Father God, because of you we need never fear what life has in store for us because you are with us. Father we are grateful that you strengthen us in our efforts for the kingdom. Lord invoke in our spirits panic when we fall short; that we may immediately remember the cross of Christ from which salvation flows then ask forgiveness. We know fear is born out of mankind's failure to be obedient to your word along with a lack of faith. Lord strengthen our faith to remove our fear. Through Christ Jesus our Lord and Savior we pray. Amen

Day 320

My God, my God, why have you forsaken me? Why are you so far from saving me, from the words of my groaning? (Psalm 22:1 ESV)

These are the words quoted by Jesus as he hung dying on the cross of Calvary. God the Father turned away from God the Son because he could not bear viewing the mantle of the worlds sin which engulfed Jesus. You and I need never think that God has forsaken us, because he said he never would. It may sometimes look like God is not near, but he is as close as speaking the name of Jesus.

Prayer: O Lord our God who is Awesome and Wonderful, there are times when we call on you and you seem so far away. Lord it is at those times that we feel abandoned by you. Lord it is at those times that the grief, frustration, loneliness, anger and pain in our lives seem insurmountable. Lord we seek your comfort and presence. Lord, give us the reassurance that you are there; no further than just a prayer away. Lord, hear our prayers in the name of the Father, Son and Holy Spirit. Amen

Day 321

and you will know the truth, and the truth will set you free." (John 8:32 ESV)

There is the philosophical truth that the earth is inhabited by both the male and female gender of each species of mammal. There is the mathematical truth that numbers cannot controvert from their true meaning to produce a sum we desire them to be. Truth stands on its own merits without wavering it is as rigid and timeless as the Rock of Gibraltar. Truth for the Christian is found in Christ Jesus. Jesus is the truth of our salvation. There is no other means of salvation for mankind other than Jesus "The Way, Truth and the Life".

Prayer: Holy and Merciful Father God, so very often we children of men slip into sin, yet we try to whitewash and diffuse the severity of our sin. Help us Lord to view sin for what it is which is a fracture in our relationship with you. Help us to repent asking that we never again repeat the same sin, no matter how small. Help us to understand that sin is sin and acknowledging this truth sets us free. Father let the truth of your grace in Christ Jesus guide us to shun sin and not be liars concerning our sinful activities. Lord, hear our prayer in Jesus' Holy and Precious name. Amen

Day 322

The Lord is my shepherd; I shall not want. (Psalm 23:1 KJV)

God demonstrates to us daily that he is a God of relationship. As the Good Shepherd, Jesus came to offer us an abundant life. We can see in this verse what Jesus does for us all the days of our lives. We also peek into the future because if we are children of God, want will not be a part of our vocabulary.

Prayer: O God our Shepherd, we want so very much to be independent, yet we like sheep are fragile and weak. LORD, help us to recognize our dependence on you. Lift us up O LORD and carry us to the safety of your bosom. We need you LORD, help us to lean on you in the name of Jesus we pray. Amen

Day 323

Give us this day our daily bread. (Matthew 6:11 KJV)

All provisions come from God Alone. Our daily bread consists of not just the foods we eat but support through our vocations, our health and strength also. It can be sustenance which is nourishment. It can be our livelihoods where we earn our money. So, when you get any of these you have it all, you have your daily bread. The slang for money is bread. This provides us with all the incidentals we require for our existence on this earth. You know the fine clothes, jewelry, the nice vehicle to ride around in, the nice house with all the furnishings; the ability to seek proper health care. When we have these things, we have our daily bread.

Prayer: Lord God our Heavenly Father, from time to time we get big eyed. Lord we desire more than is necessary because of greed. Forgive us for coveting more than our daily portion. Father God give us contentment with our daily bread. This we pray in Jesus' name. Amen

Day 324

to the only God our Savior be glory, majesty, power
and authority, through Jesus Christ our Lord, before
all ages, now and forevermore! Amen. (Jude 25 NIV)

Only God is our savior. As the Bible plainly states Jesus is the savior of the world. Therefore, this is saying that God through the incarnate body of Jesus has the power and authority and the majesty not just now but forevermore. That is eternity.

Prayer: LORD God, to you alone we offer our worship, honor and praise. You are the only God who could save us for a future with you. To you O God be glory, majesty, power and authority through Jesus Christ our Lord we pray. Amen

Day 325

Who is he that condemns? Christ Jesus, who died--more
than that, who was raised to life--is at the right hand of
God and is also interceding for us. (Romans 8:34 NIV)

While on this earth Christ taught us the ways to live in harmony with
one another. Jesus also gave us an example of living a wholesome life
directed towards heavenly principles. After Jesus left earth forty days
after his resurrection he sat down at the right hand of God the father.
From the heavenly realm Jesus in conjunction with the Holy Spirit
intercedes for us as we march towards eternity.

Prayer: Holy and Gracious Father God, we thank you for the intercession
of Christ Jesus who makes a plea on our behalf. Father move us to
intercede for one another as we follow the example of our Lord Jesus
Christ, in whose name we pray. Amen

Day 327

God is our refuge and strength, a very present help in
trouble. (Psalm 46:1 KJV)

When you feel there is no protection left for you in this world it is time
to remember That God is the shelter away from the storms of life.
Safety and courage is found in reliance on the Lord. When it appears
the world around you are falling apart, go the Jesus.

Prayer: O God our Lord, we are constantly inundated by trouble in this
world. In you alone Father God through Christ Jesus do we find comfort
for our troubled minds. O God you are our refuge and strength. LORD
as we continue towards our eternal home in Glory thank you for being
a present help in our times of trouble on this side of eternity. In Jesus'
name, we pray. Amen

Day 328

> And those who went before and those who followed
> were shouting, "Hosanna! Blessed is he who comes in
> the name of the Lord! (Mark 11:9 ESV)

Jesus, our savior, our intercessor, our calm in the storm, was recognized as he entered Jerusalem with shouts of Hosanna. That word is an acclamation of adoration. You and I should also worship, praise and be filled with joy that our God is the God who created all things and yet is aware and loving towards sinners like us.

Prayer: Father God, we come to you in the name of Jesus shouting Hosanna (We Praise You) (Save Us). Lord save us from life's temptations, fears and dangers. Lord, save us from our own stinking thinking regarding ourselves and others. Father help us to be more Christ like in thought, word and deed. In Jesus' name, we pray. Amen

Day 329

> And a second is like it: You shall love your neighbor as
> yourself. (Matthew 22:39 NRSV)

When the word love is used by Jesus in this text it is not brotherly love he is speaking of but the agape love. Agape love is filled with commitment it is sacrificial and places no conditions on its recipient. Jesus came offering Agape love as he proceeded towards Calvary's cross for all mankind. Jesus did not demand that we love him. Jesus directed us to love one another.

Prayer: LORD, hear us as we look to you for strength and ability. Help us to love those who do not look like us, speak, like us or even think like us. Father God help each of us to assist in removing the barriers of racial, ethnic, cultural and language which separate your people on earth. Father God you made all people in your image therefore we see the wonderful diversity of your handiwork in the faces of every man, woman and child on this planet. Father hear our prayer in Jesus' name. Amen

Day 330

> Not that I have already obtained all this, or have already
> been made perfect, but I press on to take hold of that
> for which Christ Jesus took hold of me. (Phil 3:12 NIV)

Our lives are a series of challenges, defeats, errors and successes. This will be, as long as we have the breath of life in our bodies on this earth. While living on this earth "we have not arrived", or in other words we are not ever going to reach the top of the hill of perfection. Please understand there is more awaiting the Christian who believes Christ Jesus died for them. Despite the slips and falls of this life, keep on pushing towards the goal of eternity with Christ. When he returns to carry us home to be with him then will perfection be obtained. In the meantime, press on.

Prayer: Lord Jesus, if we ever come to a point where we think we have an inerrant grasp of your word and who you are, humble us. Lord we will never be perfected in this life, but we can press towards the elevation of our knowledge of you through the study of your word. Lord, empower us with spiritual growth while we are yet on this side of the cross. This we pray in the name of the Father, Son and Holy Spirit. Amen

Day 331

> And I will give this people favor in the sight of the
> Egyptians; and when you go, you shall not go empty.
> (Exodus 3:21 ESV)

When you are a child of God, he can not only make your opponents be at peace with you but also generous towards you. God is the God of adjustment. When brokenness came into God's perfect creation he said through his creation, the woman's offspring would come to make it right. Do not be discouraged when it seems people are withholding what will profit you. God will provide either through them or by another means of his choosing.

Prayer: LORD God our Provider, frequently your people are found in unfavorable conditions and situations. Yet you O God cause your people who are called by your name to come out on top and not beneath. LORD we thank you for bringing us out of the worst possible condition of being out of favor with you because of sin. Thank you, LORD, for the grace given us through Christ Jesus our Lord and Savior. Amen

Day 332

O Lord, God of my salvation; I cry out day and night
before you. (Psalm 88:1 ESV)

We can appeal to the Lord God Almighty since he is our salvation. As we suffer the afflictions of living on this earth we can go to no one else who can offer the type of spiritual comfort our loving God can offer. As we go to the throne of grace with our supplications we speak out of pain asking God for relief. This we do day and night. God is ever listening and working on our behalf. Just know that he hears our cry. As we pray, it is Christ through the Holy Spirit who gives us guidance towards comfort.

Prayer: LORD God Almighty, thank you for allowing trouble to pass through our lives. It is at those trying and troubling times when we fix our eyes on you and act not out of personal resources but out of faith in you. LORD as we continue to pray our way through circumstances help us to know that Christ Jesus is there alongside you, the intercessor on our behalf. In Jesus' name, we pray. Amen

Day 333

Jesus answered, "The work of God is this: to believe in the one he has sent." (John 6:29 NIV)

How many times have you heard people say I want to do a great work for the Lord? People reflect on the lives of people such as Luther, Mother Theresa, Dr. King and people who lived during Biblical times, those who have worked for the benefit of the kingdom. Every man, woman, boy and girl can do a great work for the Lord by believing in him. God is not a man that he should lie. His promises are true and beyond doubt. Accomplishments which attain us notoriety account for nothing except to the world where people hold in high esteem those whose names are on everyone's lips. In the Lord's sight, great work is belief in his redemption of your life which was bought at a great price. Grandiosity of action compares little in God's sight to grandiosity of faith.

Prayer: LORD God who gives us life, we want so very much to work for you. For many Lord that gets twisted into thinking of having a large church or having people know your name because of some accomplishment. Father God help us to know and to share with your people your true work; which is that we believe in Christ Jesus whom you sent. This we pray in Jesus' name. Amen

Day 334

Show hospitality to one another without grumbling. (1 Peter 4:9 ESV)

Jesus taught us to be ready to share with those who have less. If someone asks something of you and it is within your power to give it, then give it. If a stranger needs shelter and you can safely provide that shelter do so. When you offer to others what they do not have, and you do have you are demonstrating love for God and the love of God.

Prayer: Lord God Heavenly Father, grumbling is a way of life for mankind and Christians are not exempt. Father the Hebrews grumbled against you in the desert after being delivered from Egypt. People grumble against one another. People grumble after you have provided salvation through Christ Jesus. Help us to refrain from grumbling as we reflect on the goodness of Christ. In Jesus' name, we pray. Amen

Day 335

I have been crucified with Christ; it is no longer I who live, but Christ lives in me; and the life which I now live in the flesh I live by faith in the Son of God, who loved me and gave Himself for me. (Galatians 2:20 NKJV)

As we attempt to live more Christlike in our daily lives, we seek to slay the carnal man and allow the spiritual man to emerge. We struggle daily with living according to Christian values. The flesh always strives to have its way. We must crucify the flesh which directs us to worldly activities. As we crucify the flesh we turn our wills and lives over to Christ who loves us and gave himself for us. Our faith should be in Christ, not sports teams or figures or celebrities or politicians or Pastors.

Prayer: Our Father in Heaven, we your hand made servants need you to enlighten us as to whom we should praise. Father, far too many people O God applaud men for their accomplishments to the point of shedding tears; yet to you they offer only mediocre praise. Father God help your people to know they are nothing and you through Christ Jesus is everything. Help us to understand that nothing should be more loved and admired than Christ. LORD, hear our prayer in Jesus, name. Amen

Day 336

and rend your hearts and not your garments. Return to the Lord, your God, for he is gracious and merciful,

slow to anger, and abounding in steadfast love; and he
relents over disaster. (Joel 2:13 ESV)

The word of God teaches us to tear not our clothing but tear our hearts.
The tearing of clothing was a sign of grief in the Ancient Near East.
We are called to grieve in our hearts for the brokenness of our sin. As
we come to God with contrite hearts he will receive us because of his
mercy and grace.

Prayer: O LORD our God, in days past men tore their garments as a
show of sorrow. Father help us to rip our hearts as a show of sorrow for
failing you time and again. Thank you, Lord God for your everlasting
gracious mercy which is represented through Christ Jesus our Lord
and Savior. Father forgive us in Jesus' name. Amen

Day 337

He will wipe away every tear from their eyes, and death
shall be no more, neither shall there be mourning nor
crying nor pain anymore, for the former things have
passed away. (Revelation 21:4 ESV)

There awaits the child of God a new life after this earthly life. Whereas
this earthly life has sorrow, pain, illness and the curse of death, the
new life to come does not. We will dwell with God in his New Jerusalem
after Jesus returns to claim his chosen people. Things will not look as
they do now nor will we experience life as we do now. The old will pass
away and the new will come.

Prayer: O God our Savior, we now live in this world where pain, sickness
and death are the result of sin. Lord you sent Jesus to comfort your
created people giving us hope for a brighter future. Father God we look
forward to the day when all tears will be wiped away. Father we look
forward to the day when there will be no more mourning and pain.
Lord we look to the day when we will come to live with you in that
prepared place for your prepared people. In Jesus' name, we pray. Amen

Day 338

Blessed are those who mourn, for they will be comforted. (Matt 5:4 NIV)

We mourn for the death of our loved ones as their time here on earth comes to an end. Over 2000 years ago there was a day of mourning for many who stood at the cross of Calvary. They mourned as Christ hung dying. They mourned as they believed that all was now lost because their leader was dying. They mourned because they did not fully understand all that Christ had taught them during his three-year ministry. Because history illuminates the past we now know that although Jesus died, three days later he rose from the dead so that we too shall one day rise from the dead unto eternal life with him. Why mourn death on this earth "The Best Is Yet to Come". Live now so that you can be raised in that new spiritual body for life in the Kingdom which was prepared since the creation of the world.

Prayer: Lord God Heavenly Father, we experience death because of sin being brought into your creation. Death leaves us with a whole that only you can fill. We miss our loved ones who die before us. Because of the blessed hope given through Jesus' resurrection we can know that one day we will see them again. Because of Jesus we are blessed. Through Jesus we pray. Amen

Day 339

Let us fix our eyes on Jesus, the author and perfecter of our faith, who for the joy set before him endured the cross, scorning its shame, and sat down at the right hand of the throne of God. (Hebrews 12:2 NIV)

In track and field, the runner has and objective which is the finish line. We also have a finish line as Christians. For the Christian, the finish line is eternity with Christ. Jesus is the object of our faith as we run the race of life. While living out our lives we go about looking to-and-fro.

Keeping our focus on the worldly is of no value. We must maintain our focus on Jesus alone.

Prayer: Lord Jesus, send the Holy Spirit to urge us to look to you the author and perfecter of our faith. Amen

Day 340

Sharon shall become a pasture for flocks, and the Valley of Achor a place for herds to lie down, for my people who have sought me. (Isaiah 65:10 ESV)

We currently live in a broken world. The world is filled with terror, deceit, hostility, illness and death. Because of the disobedience of Adam, we must labor for our sustenance. Although we may own a plot of land on this earth, we are but pilgrims passing through. Our true home awaits us in another life to come. There we will be in the presence of our Savior God. There we will have all we need to live in abundant joy.

Prayer: Heavenly Father God, although many do not understand the concept of a pasture we thank you for the pasture of your grace, mercy and love. Lord a pasture is a place of reproducing supply. As the cattle and flocks eat the grass which nourishes them their food supply continues to grow under their feet. Thank you, Lord God that you arranged to bring us to green pasture through Christ Jesus our shepherd. In Jesus' name, we pray. Amen

Day 341

Now faith is the substance of things hoped for, the evidence of things not seen. (Hebrews 11:1 KJV)

You do not hope for what you already have. Hope is based on the unseen. Belief is faith in action; confidence that the unseen will fashion into a material reality. What the mind of faith can conceive the manifestation of faith can achieve. Believe it and receive it.

Prayer: Lord God Almighty, we wait with bated breath for what you have in store for us in our future. Father God your promises are true because you cannot lie. Help us to patiently wait for the fulfillment of what faith says we now possess, although it is not now visible. In Jesus' name, we pray. Amen

Day 342

> May the God who gives endurance and encouragement
> give you a spirit of unity among yourselves as you
> follow Christ Jesus. (Romans 15:5 NIV)

There is much division in the Christian community because of varying doctrinal views. The truth is, none really know what the entire truth is. Unless it aligns with scripture aside from man's contribution, it is questionable. People say scripture is left to individual interpretation. That is far from the truth. Only through the Spirit of God can scripture be properly interpreted. We must seek to dissolve the barriers that separate the church on earth, so that unity may exist among God's precious people.

Prayer: Lord God of comfort, thank you for the comfort of your presence in our daily lives. Help us O God to comfort one another with the same compassion you have shown us. Help us Lord to have unity of spirit, fellowship in the word and unified worship for you. In Jesus' name, we pray. Amen

Day 343

> Now the God of hope fill you with all joy and peace in
> believing, that ye may abound in hope, through the
> power of the Holy Ghost. (Romans 15:13 KJV)

Hope looks forward with expectation. Hope is a result of the power of the Holy Spirit. People cannot conjure up hope in their own power due to the minds rejection of that which is not visible. In our anticipation of what God has in store for us after the resurrection, we can be filled with peace of mind joy as we accept that God's word is truth. Allow the encouragement of the Holy Spirit to overshadow you as you await a vibrant future with God for ever and ever.

Prayer: LORD God the Father of our Lord and Savior Jesus Christ, we thank you for the hope which is provided through Christ Jesus. Thank you for the peace of our weary conscience as the Holy Spirit strengthens our faith in our march towards eternity. In Jesus' name, we pray. Amen

Day 344

After this he went out and saw a tax collector named Levi, sitting at the tax booth. And he said to him, "Follow me." (Luke 5:27 ESV)

Jesus comes to us as he did to Levi the outcast tax collector and says to us, "Follow Me". This is not an invitation but a command. This command will lead us into a brighter future if we heed it. If we choose to disregard it, we will be doomed to an eternity outside of the presence of God.

Prayer: Lord Jesus, help us to hear and act as you invite us as you say, "Follow Me". Help us Lord to pursue you with an unyielding passion. This we pray in the name of the Father Son and Holy Spirit. Amen

Day 345

"I am the good shepherd; I know my sheep and my sheep know me. (John 10:14 NIV)

Following the shepherd often means some very steep climbs up rough and dangerous paths. Following the shepherd means leaving the safety of the sheep fold and going out among watching and waiting dangers. The sheep couldn't always see the shepherd and that can panic sheep. There is however the opportunity to listen to his voice which comforts the uneasy and the frightened. When you are rooted in Christ, there is a deep knowledge of him and you can decipher his voice amid the chaos of this world.

Prayer: Good Shepherd, we know you lead us in the paths of righteousness and you protect us to the point of offering your very life. Thank you, Lord thank you in the name of Jesus. Amen

Day 346

But as for you, be strong and do not give up, for your
work will be rewarded. (2 Chronicles 15:7 NIV)

The Bible speaks of a reward awaiting those who persevere until the last day. That perseverance is maintaining your faith in Christ Jesus until your last breath on this earth. Jesus has promised to those who endure to the end even in view of persecution from the prince of this world a crown of life. Be strong and do not give up.

Prayer: Heavenly Father God, we children of men want so very much in our inward being to work the work you have called us to. LORD give us strength so that we do not give up in carrying out our daily assignments. This we ask in Jesus' name. Amen

Day 347

Blessed shall you be when you come in and blessed
shall you be when you go out. (Deuteronomy 28:6 ESV)

God has you covered when you come and when you go. God showers blessing on His faithful people. As you move throughout life blessing will follow you and blessings will meet you wherever you go. All too often we become desensitized to the numerous blessings of God and often look at the blessings of life as privileges rather than gifts of God. Take one day and count your blessings. Begin with knowing who you are when you awaken and the use of your extremities and senses.

Prayer: Lord God our Heavenly Father, so that we are worthy of the blessings you have planned for us in your covenant with mankind, empower us to walk in the light of your word that we give honor to you in everything we do. Help us to be grateful for your benevolent gifts. In Jesus' name we pray. Amen

Day 348

> "And if you faithfully obey the voice of the Lord your God, being careful to do all his commandments that I command you today, the Lord your God will set you high above all the nations of the earth. (Deuteronomy 28:1 ESV)

The wonderful thing about the commands of God is that they give us step by step guidance as we proceed through the minefield of life. This world has dangers that are ever present. Some dangers are external; some are of our own making. From Genesis to Revelation God has given us instruction on how to live as His people. When you live as a child of God you are set apart from the rest of the world.

Prayer: O Lord our God and Creator, as we hear your voice we seek to obey you Lord. Lord in the name of Jesus we want to do all you command yet our ears seem attuned to the world and its values. Help us O God today to live out your commandments shutting out the worldly and embracing the eternal. Lord in your mercy, hear our prayer. In Jesus' name we pray. Amen

Day 349

> This they said to test him, that they might have some charge to bring against him. Jesus bent down and wrote with his finger on the ground. (John 8:6 ESV)

It is said that Jesus is a mighty good lawyer. A woman was brought before Him who was sentenced to death for the act of adultery. The Pharisees were adamant about having her executed by stoning. When they asked Jesus His opinion he stooped down and began to use His finger to write in the dirt. Jesus was demonstrating that we all get some dirt on us either by choice or by circumstance. The world is a dirty place. Only by the blood of Jesus can we become clean again.

Prayer: Lord you alone are our awesome wonderful and Mighty God, we thank you Lord for bending down from heaven to lift us from the mire in the pit of sin. Where would we be if not for you? Father in Jesus' name let us do likewise towards one another while we are yet on this side of the cross. Lord, hear our prayer in Jesus' name. Amen

Day 351

> For God alone my soul waits in silence; from him comes my salvation. (Psalm 62:1 ESV)

Confidence in God as Savior is paramount to the Christian way of life. We know through Scripture that we cannot save ourselves from a burning hell only the precious blood of Jesus can do that for us. When we are rooted in the Lord our personality demonstrates that there is something inside that is so strong, which enables us to walk through what consumes those who do not have a relationship with Jesus.

Prayer: Heavenly Father our God, we come in the name of Jesus expressing our confidence in the salvation which is found in you through Christ alone. Lord, our trust is in your plan for our deliverance. In Jesus' name we pray. Amen

Day 352

He gives power to the faint and strengthens the
powerless. (Isaiah 40:29 NRSV)

We like to think of ourselves as being strong. This is seen in people
who frequent gyms for weight training lifting tremendous amounts of
weight to show they have strong muscles. We are but delicate fragile
humans who are here on this earth but for a short period of time. It is
by God's power that we are found to be strong in faith and for some
in deeds. Ask Jesus to strengthen your feeble mind, body and soul.
Through Him you can receive strength.

Prayer: O God our Heavenly Father, we are weak, but you are strong.
Lord in our weakened condition you looked upon those who called
upon you and gave them strength. Thank you, Lord, for strengthening
us by coming as the man Jesus Christ as you saw us in our feeble
circumstance. We thank and praise you in Jesus' name. Amen

Day 353

Blessed is he whose transgression is forgiven, whose
sin is covered. (Psalm 32:1 NKJV)

When you place your faith in Christ Jesus and then transgress through
thought, word or deed, you can come to Jesus and ask for forgiveness.
All we do is ask in true repentance then in His faithfulness, He will
remove the stain of sin away from us. What a blessing it is to have the
Lamb of God take away our sin by covering us in His blood.

Prayer: Lord God Who Forgives, we children of men can go about life
with exuberant joy because regardless of our lives being stained by
the sin of this world you view us in the shadow of the cross and offer
forgiveness. Thank you, Lord God for the cleansing offered through the
blood of Christ Jesus in whose name we pray. Amen

Day 354

How much more severely do you think a man deserves
to be punished who has trampled the Son of God under
foot, who has treated as an unholy thing the blood of
the covenant that sanctified him, and who has insulted
the Spirit of grace? (Hebrews 10:29 NIV)

Is Jesus garbage to be trampled underfoot? Jesus shed His precious
blood for all mankind that we, each one now has an opportunity for
eternal life. After we leave this existence God has another existence
prepared for those who accept Jesus as Lord and savior. This next
existence in paradise is not awaiting those who seek to crush the
sacrificial act of Jesus' suffering and death. Those who identify Jesus as
just another dead corpse and not accepting His rising from the dead
insult God's Holy Spirit which teaches all truth to the fertile heart.

Prayer: Holy Spirit of Grace, forgive us if mistakenly minimalize
the Holy Sanctifying Blood of Christ Jesus as we go about our daily
activities. Help us to not trample underfoot our Savior in our haste to
be productive in this life. Help us to give the Blood of Jesus its proper
place at the pinnacle of all we say, think and do. Lord in your Mercy
hear our Prayer. Amen

Day 355

See to it that no one misses the grace of God and that
no bitter root grows up to cause trouble and defile
many. (Hebrews 12:15 NIV)

God extends His grace to any who seek it. Many people who are
walking in the darkness of this sin sick world think it is up to them
through self-actuation to change their lives. Only the Spirit of the
Living God can change the heart of a person with that mindset. That
type of person is operating through the bitter roots of pride, bitterness
and anything else that separates people from coming to Christ Jesus

to receive the grace He has offered us. Allow the Spirit of God to work in you so people will see and experience God's grace in their lives as it flows through you.

Prayer: Holy Lord our God who forgives, we children of men fight a never-ending battle as the overseer of our heart. Lord we allow anger, resentment and retaliation to take residence there which breeds bitterness and sin. Lord God Almighty help us replace the destructive thoughts with constructive action as we remember how Christ gave his all as an act which gained us mercy. Help us O God to be attentive to our hearts; guarding them against the evil which would dwell there. Father God hear our prayer we ask in Jesus' name. Amen

Day 356

And the free gift is not like the result of that one man's sin. For the judgment following one trespass brought condemnation, but the free gift following many trespasses brought justification. (Romans 5:16 ESV)

Through Adam we are immersed in original sin. Because of original sin we are conceived in sin and born sinful. All mankind faces condemnation because of the act of Adam as he became disobedient in the Garden of Eden. Fortunately for mankind God is merciful. God told Satan that although he seduced Eve who then enticed her husband Adam to disobey God's command, not the eat the fruit of the tree of the "knowledge of good and evil". God said He would return as a human to crush Satan's efforts. Jesus came into the world as the incarnate God from heaven who brought with Him the "free gift" of salvation, to all who would receive it. Irrespective of our original and actual sin Jesus came and validated us before a Holy God.

Prayer: God of Grace, our lips speak praise to you for the wonderful gift of salvation given through the "free gift" offered by Christ Jesus which brought justification to all mankind. Lord, hear our prayer in Jesus' name. Amen

Day 357

Your words were found, and I ate them, and your
words became to me a joy and the delight of my heart,
for I am called by your name, O Lord, God of hosts.
(Jeremiah 15:16 NRSV)

When you receive the word of God through scripture either preached,
prayed or sung your heart fills with joy for the love demonstrated to
you through Jesus. You take the word of God in just as you do with
nourishing food. You absorb the word and make it a part of your life.
As you grow more spiritual by the word, you turn your will and your
life over to the care of God through Christ Jesus. When you do this, you
are called a "Child of God".

Prayer: Lord God of Hosts, we found your words and as we consumed
them our lives became enriched. Lord God Almighty, the words
brought joy to our hearts and enlightenment to our minds. O Lord,
we are your children, blood bought by Christ Jesus, sanctified and
called by your name. Thank you in Jesus' name. Amen

Day 358

"Be still and know that I am God. I will be exalted
among the nations; I will be exalted in the earth!"
(Psalm 46:10 NKJV)

When the predicaments, uncertainties and anxieties of this world
collide with our tranquility we must make a choice. When the hustle
and bustle of worldly concerns come. When you feel left alone by family
and friends. When the devil attacks seeking to shake your serenity.
Open your spiritual ears and hear God's voice breaking through
the calamity. God speaks to His hard pressed, frazzled and shaken
children saying, "Be still, and know that I am God". In saying this
God is saying because your faith is rooted in my son Jesus, remember
He has carried all your worries, woes, isolation and fears to Calvary.

People will see in you an unfaltering steadfastness that only I can give. All of this will one day come to completion when Jesus returns to claim a harvest of those saved and sanctified believers who are awaiting His return.

Prayer: Lord God of Comfort and Peace, in this hectic world we your children can easily become agitated by the events of life. Father God help us to be still and know that you are God all by yourself. Lord, help us to invest in the quiet time of Bible Study, Prayer and meditation which gives us pause to experience your peace. In Jesus' precious name we pray. Amen

Day 356

Do your best to present yourself to God as one approved, a worker who has no need to be ashamed, rightly handling the word of truth. (2 Tim. 2:15 ESV)

When you open your mouth attempting to direct people to Christ be sure what you are saying can be supported by scripture. Often in our effort to share the Good News people say things that might sound scriptural yet cannot be supported by God's word. In your attempt to witness to the Gospel of Jesus Christ never use the term I know that is in the Bible unless you can take the person directly to that Book, Chapter and Verse. The only way to Know God's Word is to Study God's Word. Hallelujah's and Praise you Jesus's can come out of your mouth all day long. That does not make you knowledgeable of scripture, only study brings you into God's realm. If you do not know the Word, then how can you share it? Study to show yourself approved; as one who knows the word.

Prayer: Lord God the strength of the needy, many are the times when we pursue empty activities like sporting events, television and idle chat on the telephone which profit us nothing. Father God these empty activities keep us from spending time with you. LORD, renew the thinking of your people that their minds can be stayed on you and your

Word become the more sought-after activity. LORD, hear our prayer in Jesus' name. Amen

Day 357

> O God, you are my God, earnestly I seek you; my soul thirsts for you, my body longs for you, in a dry and weary land where there is no water. (Psalm 63:1 NIV)

There is only one true God, He is the creator of the heavens and the earth and all that lies within. God is Elohim the supreme God of all things. As we open our eyes to see the beginning of a brand-new day, we should seek His face through acknowledgement of His presence in our lives as the first thing on our daily agenda. If you do not make God first other things will distract you and divert your attention away from His guidance for your day. As a person who is parched and dry in a desert would seek after a drink of water, let that be your early morning focus for God in your life.

Prayer: Father God, we live in an arid wilderness land parched by pain, discord, sickness and death. Father God it is only through the life-giving water of Christ that we are sustained, comforted and refreshed. We thank you O God that Jesus has met us in this desert place. In Jesus name we offer our heartfelt gratitude. Amen

Day 358

> Moreover, when God gives any man wealth and possessions, and enables him to enjoy them, to accept his lot and be happy in his work, this is a gift of God. (Ecclesiastes 5:19 NIV)

God gives us all things. We must remember that God's gifts are good since every good and perfect gift comes from God (**James 1:17**). It is God who gives us the ability to obtain wealth (**Deuteronomy 8:18**). We have the activity of our limbs along with being clothed in our right minds, so we may enjoy what God has provided. Accept your work as a gift from God and joy will fill your heart.

Prayer: Most Hallowed God our Father, all we have has been given by you. Lord our wealth, possessions, authority and lives we owe to you alone. Thank you, LORD, for the gifts you have provided in this life. We want to thank you most of all for your very best gift of Christ Jesus the sacrificial Lamb of God who died that we might receive salvation. In Jesus' name we pray. Amen

Day 359

Multitudes, multitudes, in the valley of decision! For the day of the Lord is near in the valley of decision. (Joel 3:14 NIV)

Judgment is coming upon this world. All who have lived in this world will one day stand before the judgement seat of God. When called before God's judgement seat will have to give an account of our lives. For some this will be a day of joy as we confess Christ Jesus through whom we have been made righteous. For others who rejected Jesus it will be a day of mourning and regret. And we must remember there will also be a third group who walked the earth deceiving people into thinking they lived holy lives but secretly lived for the worldly passion available. Jesus will on that day say, "welcome to some and away to others".

Prayer: Lord God the Judge of all the earth, Lord you judge with impunity because you allowed Jesus to carry our sins to the cross due to your great love for us. Thank you, Lord God for life which flows from you. Help the peoples of the earth to decide to follow Christ Jesus, the one who paid the blood ransom that they might receive eternal life. In Jesus' name we pray. Amen.

Day 360

The Lord bless you and keep you. (Numbers 6:24 NIV)

It need not be said because it already is. It began with the incident in the garden as the LORD the Almighty God spoke a prophetic word concerning the future of mankind to the serpent. "The seed of the woman will crush your head". It was reinforced at a hill called Calvary on one Friday evening when Jesus gave His life for mankind. It was confirmed three days later when the tomb Jesus was laid in was found to be empty. The empty tomb showed that because Jesus rose from the dead we too shall one day rise to eternal life. You are Blessed!

Prayer: Lord God Almighty, our only means of thanking you for your many blessings is to offer our love, care, mercy and forgiveness to one another. Help us Father God bless and not condemn. Lord, help us to elevate and not put down. Thank you, Lord for your blessings and eternal favor which was given through Christ Jesus. We pray in Jesus' name. Amen

Day 361

All scripture is given by inspiration of God, and is profitable for doctrine, for reproof, for correction, for instruction in righteousness. (2 Timothy 3:16 KJV)

You may hear some say the bible was written by men, that is true. But what those individuals do not say is that the men who wrote the Bible were inspire by God who enables them to write those scriptures. God used the distinctive style and vocabulary of each writer because God's purpose and plan needed to be presented through the words of ordinary men. God's supernatural influence penned the words of the Bible by the hands of men. Men wrote through God's anointing, so mankind could gain wisdom, become edified in proper living, be corrected and turned around where sin flourished and be guided by God's directives, so virtue would abound.

Prayer: O LORD our God, we experience many different facets of life as we march from the womb to the tomb. Thank you, Father God for your Word both written and incarnate. It is the Word O God which gives us direction when we do not know which way to turn. Help us to keep our focus on the Word in our thoughts, words and deeds. In Jesus Day' name we pray. Amen

Day 362

It is better to trust in the LORD than to put confidence in princes. (Psalm 118:9 KJV)

People venerate other human beings and exalt them to earthly altars of worship. If another human being has the same frailties as you, such as being prone to deception, illness and death why venerate them. The only human being to ever walk the earth with the power of salvation in His hands was Jesus. No Bishop, Pastor, Pope, president or politician can save your eternal soul. Jesus is the only one with that authority. Trust in Jesus alone all others will fail you.

Prayer: Lord God our Heavenly Father, we your children will frequently ask other men and women for assistance only to be let down. Man has the tendency to say one thing and act in another manner. Other human beings often let us down, but you never do. Thank you, Lord God that you alone can be fully trusted to keep your word. Thank you, Father for the Word which bought us life, His name is Jesus. In Jesus' name we pray. Amen

Day 363

Order my steps in thy word: and let not any iniquity have dominion over me. (Psalm 119:133 KJV)

When we allow our lives to be guided by the word of God our steps will be ordered. This suggests we will be disciplined as we go about our daily lives. An ordered person in Christ restricts the type of words which proceeds from their mouths. An ordered person exercises Christian directed judgement in their actions towards other people they meet. An ordered person makes every thought subject to Christ, that they may be pure and undefiled. Ask the Lord through prayer to order your steps in His Word.

Prayer: Lord God Almighty our Heavenly Father, as a symphony orchestra director uses his baton to direct the movement of each piece of music to create a beautiful; moving selection direct my actions through your word to allow me to be a completed work which gives glory to you and which gives pleasure to those with whom I come in contact. In Jesus' name we pray. Amen

Day 364

Even before a word is on my tongue, behold, O Lord,
you know it altogether. (Psalm 139:4 ESV)

God knows us intimately. God knew us as we were being constructed in our mother's womb and because of that He knows our end even before our beginning. God knows us so thoroughly that before the words of our mouths are spoken He already knows them. God is answering our prayers before we ask. God knows our needs before we open our mouths to speak of them.

Prayer: Heavenly Father God, before we approach you in prayer you know the words which are stored up in our hearts. Thank you, LORD for knowing us so intimately and lovingly. In Jesus' name we pray. Amen

Day 365

O Lord, I say to you, "You are my God." Hear, O Lord,
my cry for mercy. (Psalm 140:6 NIV)

Lord, we know that nothing good lives inside of us. We are all in need of your mercy daily. Lord, there are times we need your mercy minute by minute because of the sin which resides in us. Lord in your mercy hear us as we boldly tell you, that we don't want ill speech to proceed from our lips of clay. Lord, we look at what we know is not pleasing to you. Lord we do not make every thought subject to Christ. Lord, please do not allow the sinful nature to overtake and govern us. Lord in your mercy, guide us to the better way of life.

Prayer: O LORD our God, we approach you in the name of Jesus saying you alone are our God. Forgive us LORD God for placing anything before you in our lives. O God it is through you that we live and have the opportunity to interact with one another. LORD in your mercy, help us with the sin that so easily ensnare us. LORD in your mercy; hear our plea for mercy and your continued grace. In Jesus' name we pray. Amen

Day 366

And when the devil had ended every temptation, he departed from him until an opportune time. (Luke 4:13 ESV)

The devil has an agenda. His days are short in the scheme of things when compared to eternity. He wants company in that place which is prepared for him and his followers. As Winston Churchill once said, "Never give in". The devil will never give up or give in on trying to motivate your spiritual slip and you succumbing to his will. As the adage goes "misery likes company". The devil is miserable in knowing that he will never enter the kingdom God has prepared for his prepared people. Are you one of God's prepared people, prepared in Christ Jesus for eternity?

Prayer: Lord God our Rock and Shield, we are under constant attack by our adversary the Devil. Lord as we battle against his temptations, illness and lure to sin, relief from his onslaught is only temporary.

He returns again and again relentlessly. Father God keep a hedge of protection around us. Father keep the name of Jesus ever upon our lips. Help us to pray for one another that we have the spiritual strength to stand against this assault. Let your Word guide and protect us. This we pray in the name of the Father, Son and the Holy Spirit. Amen

Printed in the United States
By Bookmasters